SHIPWRECKS
ALONG
LAKE SUPERIOR'S
NORTH SHORE

A DIVER'S GUIDE

SHIPWRECKS
ALONG
LAKE SUPERIOR'S
NORTH SHORE

STEPHEN B. DANIEL

MINNESOTA HISTORICAL SOCIETY PRESS

Portions of this book first appeared, in different form, in the workbook *Shipwrecks along the Minnesota North Shore: A Great Lakes Shipwreck Preservation Society Project* by Stephen B. Daniel.

www.mhspress.org

The Minnesota Historical Society Press is a member
of the Association of American University Presses.

Book and cover design: Zan Ceeley, Trio Bookworks

Cover photo credits: front (from top, left to right), Tamara Thomsen, Ken Merryman, Ron Johnson, Andrew Leidel, Jerry Eliason, (*Hesper* inset) Minnesota Historical Society/State Historic Preservation Office, Ken Merryman, Ken Merryman, Lake Superior Maritime Collection, University of Wisconsin–Superior. Back cover (top to bottom): Tamara Thomsen, Phil Kerber.

Photo on title page spread is by Tamara Thomsen from the *Madeira* shipwreck.

Manufactured in the United States

10 9 8 7 6 5 4 3 2 1

♾ The paper used in this publication meets the minimum requirements of the American National Standard for Information Sciences—Permanence for Printed Library Materials, ANSI Z39.48-1984.

International Standard Book Numbers
ISBN 13: 978-0-87351-618-1 (paper)
ISBN 10: 0-87351-618-4 (paper)

Library of Congress Cataloging-in-Publication Data

Daniel, Stephen B.
    Shipwrecks along Lake Superior's North Shore : a diver's guide / Stephen B. Daniel.
        p. cm.
    Portions of this book first appeared, in different form, in the workbook: Shipwrecks along the
Minnesota North Shore : a Great Lakes Shipwreck Preservation Society project / by Stephen B. Daniel.
    Includes bibliographical references and index.
    ISBN-13: 978-0-87351-618-1 (paper : alk. paper)
    ISBN-10: 0-87351-618-4 (paper : alk. paper)
    1. Shipwrecks—Superior, Lake—Guidebooks. 2. Shipwrecks—Minnesota—Guidebooks.
3. Historic sites—Superior, Lake—Guidebooks. 4. Historic sites—Minnesota—Guidebooks.
5. Superior, Lake—Antiquities—Guidebooks. 6. Minnesota—Antiquities—Guidebooks.
7. Underwater archaeology—Superior, Lake—Guidebooks. 8. Scuba diving—Superior, Lake—
Guidebooks. I. Daniel, Stephen B., Shipwrecks along the Minnesota North Shore. II. Great Lakes
Shipwreck Preservation Society. III. Title.
F612.S9D36 2008
917.74'90444—dc22
                                                                        2008000028

To my beloved wife, Cheri, and our children, Jeff, Corey, and Ami.
Our grown children are certified divers who enjoy the underwater sport with me.
Although not a diver, Cheri is a strong supporter of our diving activity.

Contents

Disclaimer of Liability

Scuba diving can be very dangerous and demanding recreation and may involve serious injury or death. The user of this book acknowledges both an understanding of and an assumption of the risks involved in scuba diving.

This book is intended to provide recreational divers with some general information about diving sites in order to help them have a safe and enjoyable time. This book is presented with the understanding that the author, the Great Lakes Shipwreck Preservation Society, and the publisher disclaim any responsibility with respect to the completeness or accuracy of the information provided and will not be liable with respect to any claim, action, or proceeding relating to any injury, death, loss of property, or damage to property caused or alleged to be caused, directly or indirectly, by the information contained in or omitted from this book whether caused by negligence or otherwise.

The information contained in this book is supplied merely for the convenience of the reader and must not be the only source of information for the dive sites described in this book. The author has endeavored to ensure the information contained in this book is accurate; however, the user is cautioned that environmental conditions change constantly, and the information supplied may be incorrect or incomplete on the day of any given dive. Users of this book and their dive buddies must evaluate for themselves the potential risks and dangers of each dive listed. This includes the accuracy, suitability, and applicability of all information, in addition to the availability of adequate or appropriate emergency services.

Divers should be certified, trained, and experienced for the type of diving activity they intend to do. They should also make certain their equipment is up-to-date, well-maintained, and appropriate for the intended type of diving. Many of the dives noted in the beginning of the book tend to be in shallow waters. As the book proceeds, shipwrecks will be found at deeper locations.

In the event an emergency should occur, the following action steps should be considered as appropriate. The author, the Great Lakes Shipwreck Preservation Society, and the publisher assume no liability for actions taken by divers who use this book.

General Emergencies

- On shore: Begin the First Aid ABCs and have someone call 911 and report the diving emergency.
- Aboard a boat: Begin the First Aid ABCs and have someone call the U.S. Coast Guard for assistance on a Marine Band Radio. Channel 16 is generally monitored by the U.S. Coast Guard.

At the time this book went to press, hospitals could be found in the major cities along the North Shore (Duluth, Two Harbors, and Grand Marais). They may have urgent care facilities available. Remember to call 911 for emergencies, to assure the right care is available at the time you need it.

Diver Emergencies

- Begin the First Aid ABCs and have someone report the emergency as noted above.
- Begin the First Aid ABCs, and have someone call DAN (Divers Alert Network, 919-684-8111), report the situation, and respond with care as advised by DAN medical personnel.

At the time this book went to press, the nearest hyperbaric chamber was located at Hennepin County Medical Center in Minneapolis. The hours of operation with staff present need to be confirmed before transportation to the chamber is considered. Emergency personnel, especially from DAN, will be in the best position to recommend appropriate action in this regard.

Preface

THERE ARE SHIPWRECKS located in and near just about every town along the North Shore of Lake Superior. Many of these wrecks have not been found. Shipwreck hunters do online research as well as visit historical maritime archives at a number of museums around the Great Lakes. They also go out on the water with equipment like side-scan sonar, depth finders, and underwater drop cameras. Boats tow scuba divers on underwater sleds at slow speeds; divers also ride underwater scooters. Perhaps some day we will hear news about the discovery of the *Belle Cross*, *Isle Royale*, or *Mary Martini*! Meanwhile, divers need up-to-date resources, like this book, to enable them to safely explore and enjoy known shipwrecks.

During the course of researching and writing this book, I spoke with numerous people in the diving community, as well as nondivers, regarding their interest in a guide to the shipwrecks along the North Shore of Lake Superior. They told me that, while there were sources that described sinking events and general locations of shipwrecks, they wanted more precision. It is not unusual for divers to spend a tank of air looking for a shipwreck and having to return to shore or the boat in frustration after failing to find it underwater. There were also many dive sites where things happened, but the divers who found the wreckage were reluctant to share the information with others. They were concerned that artifacts might be taken from the sites. I learned from these conversations that a more comprehensive resource was needed.

This book is intended to be a guide not only for divers to find historic shipwrecks underwater but also for nondivers who want to learn more about the ships that rest on the lake bottom. This guide is organized to provide a brief history of the ship, the story of its sinking, how the wreck site may be accessed, and what underwater visitors may expect to see. It is worth noting that while many underwater photographs may depict portions of a shipwreck, it is virtually impossible to capture the entire wreck in one image. This is because visibility in Lake Superior is often limited to thirty feet or less. On a rare occasion, such as a dry season, the visibility can be as great as seventy feet.

This necessitated a different way to show the entire ship. I made drawings underwater and after dives to record portions of a shipwreck, and then assembled the pieces in an artistic representation of the whole shipwreck. Often it took me many dives to gather the visual information so that it could be combined in a proportionate drawing. Personally diving each shipwreck was important to be able to represent it properly. You will find my shipwreck drawings and a few created by others throughout this book.

I have combined photographs of entry points with new maps that were drawn to guide visitors to a dive site. I have provided GPS coordinates, when available, to help pinpoint a location. Today, additional help is provided by the Great Lakes Shipwreck Preservation Society (GLSPS) through the placement of mooring buoys on several popular shipwrecks. These improvements have made diving easier and more enjoyable by reducing the time needed to search for the shipwreck.

I relied on two excellent resources for information about many ships and wrecking events described in this book. I am especially grateful for the research conducted by the late Dr. Julius F. Wolff and his book, *Lake Superior Shipwrecks*. I recommend that readers peruse this enlightening publication to learn more about the history of the sinkings. Another valuable resource was the book *Shipwreck!* by David D. Swayze. This often served as a resource to cross-check wreck sites as well as dates and ship dimensions for their building data and launch events. While it took more than six years to compile and write this book, these references helped save considerable time, since the authors had researched many historical sources for information related to the ships and the events that occurred to cause their destruction.

Self-contained underwater breathing apparatus (scuba) technology has vastly improved over the years.

Diver training and new equipment, such as closed-circuit rebreather systems have been developed. This equipment, along with the required training, enables experienced technical divers to descend to depths that an open-circuit air or Trimix system, such as pressurized cylinders, will not support. One of the shipwrecks described in the book requires dives down to 360 feet. The required decompression stops on the way back to the surface add hours onto the dive. Diver training and sport diving equipment have also improved. This allows safer pursuit of this fascinating sport.

Divers can enjoy reading about different shipwrecks and selecting some to consider for a weekend of diving. The drawings and details of the shipwreck will aid in planning a dive that will enable visitors to observe distinctive features they will not want to miss. Readers who want to enjoy the shipwrecks without actually visiting them on-site may study the historic photographs and underwater pictures to compare features that were evident on the ship. The drawings of the wreck on the lake bottom will show where artifacts may be seen today.

Readers may also use their imaginations to enter a shipwreck, such as the *Samuel P. Ely* in Two Harbors—"swimming" from the open bow section through the cargo hold and up through a cargo hatch near the stern. The keelson of the large ship may serve as a guide to direct the visitor down the center of the ship. By looking up at each side under the deck, the reader may "observe" knees that support the deck ledges on each side. The underwater photograph of a knee will show what one actually looks like. Enjoy the images of ships during their service on the Great Lakes. Read on to find out what happened to them and where they came to rest on the bottom of Lake Superior.

The following are the dive ratings used in this book; readers who are considering a dive can use the rating to determine if they have the appropriate skills and experience:

Novice: Beginning diver, certified for Open Water Diver, with minimal experience. Depth may be down to 60 feet.

Intermediate: A diver certified for Advanced Open Water Diver, with many dives completed. Depth may be down to 100 feet.

Advanced: A diver certified for Advanced Open Water Diver and specialty diving, such as Wreck Diver and Nitrox Diver, with several years of numerous dives at varying depths. Depth may be down to 130 feet, the maximum limit for sport diving.

Technical: A diver certified for Advanced Nitrox, Decompression Procedures, Extended Range, Trimix, and Advanced Trimix Diver, with extensive experience of deep diving over several years. Depth may be down over 130 feet.

Acknowledgments

Without the generous help of many individuals and organizations this book would not have been possible. I am particularly grateful to Scott Anfinson, of the State Historic Preservation Office of the Minnesota Historical Society (MHS), for granting permission to use images of several underwater shipwreck drawings. These drawings were created by the Tidal Atlantic Research Group during a project for MHS. I am also grateful to C. Patrick Labadie for granting permission to use images of many historic photographs from his private collection. I especially appreciate the permission granted by the Lake Superior Marine Museum Association and all the generous efforts of Laura Jacobs, archivist for the library at the University of Wisconsin–Superior, to find numerous historic photographs and grant permission to reprint them. Thom Holden was helpful in providing historical data for the old harbor, Sophie's shipwreck (the *Amethyst*), the *USS Essex*, and other ships that once sailed the Great Lakes, for which I am grateful.

I sincerely appreciate the generosity of Robert Graham, archivist for the Historical Collections of the Great Lakes at Bowling Green State University, in providing several historic images of ships; Mary Milin, of the Milwaukee Public Library, for historic ship photos; and Dr. Matthew Daley, curator of the Father Edward J. Dowling Marine Historical Collection at the University of Detroit Mercy, for the historical images he provided. I also appreciate the support from the Port Huron Museum, Great Lakes Historical Society, and Great Lakes Shipwreck Historical Society through their contributions of historic images for the book. Dorothy King was gracious in providing permission to use historic train photos by her late husband, Frank, which helped illustrate some of the stories.

I am grateful to the following organizations for providing permission to use historic photographs of ships from their collections: Bay Area Historical Society, Cook County Historical Society, Lake County Historical Society, Schroeder Area Historical Society, and St. Louis County Historical Society. I also appreciate the permission granted to use historic maritime photographs from the collections of the Northeast Minnesota Historical Center, Duluth Public Library, and the Douglas County Historical Society.

Rich Sve graciously loaned me a historic photograph of the *Madeira* salvage operation on Little Two Harbors Island, along with photographs of the removal of one of the anchors from the *Madeira*, and granted permission to reprint them. Rich also provided helpful information on the *Madeira* salvage operation. While the anchor removal photos were not ultimately used in this book, they were helpful in giving me an understanding of a salvage method used in the 1960s. Walter Sve graciously allowed us to depart from his dock to look for the schooner anchor.

Ken Merryman was generous in the use of his boat, the *Heyboy*, to dive the *Amboy, Spencer, Lafayette, A. C. Adams, Mayflower,* and *Thomas Wilson* shipwrecks. Ken also provided numerous anecdotes about several shipwrecks and some ships that have gone missing. It was a treat to participate in shipwreck hunts for the *Belle Cross* (Tim Tamlyn and I had fun scootering around the Gooseberry Reef) and the *Mary Martini*, where I planed ninety feet below the surface of Lake Superior behind the *Heyboy* near the Brule River. Ken generously provided excellent and valuable video that documented the *Mayflower* and *Wilson* when I was unable to accompany him on one of the best days to dive these wrecks.

A special thanks to Ken Merryman, Bob Olson, and Ron Benson, who dove the newly discovered *Thomas Friant* and recorded the event with both surface and underwater camera footage. Ron's boat, the *Alma*, provided the base of operations for the dive team and support crew.

Randy Beebe was very helpful in showing me the location of the *M. C. Neff* so that I could document this lumber hooker, which sank in the St. Louis River. He was generous in allowing me to use an image of his drawing of the *Onoko* shipwreck and underwater photos of the recently discovered *Harriet B.* shipwreck. He also led the Sugarloaf Cove underwater survey project, which was a unique dive experience. Nigel Wattris, captain of the *Blue Heron*, generously provided the side-scan sonar images of the *Harriet B.* shipwreck that his crew obtained when they discovered it while conducting a geological survey of the bottom of Lake Superior.

I especially appreciated Tamara Thomsen's generous contribution of time, expertise, and equipment to produce the wonderful underwater photos shown in several places in the book. Her photos exhibit superb quality, creative composition, and—most important—an outstanding representation of the intrigue and excitement that Great Lakes shipwrecks provide to divers and nondivers who view them.

My dive buddies, Bob Nelson, Byron Meyer, and my son Corey Daniel, often made themselves available to check out dive sites we had heard or read about. Bob's boat was of great benefit in reaching many of the dive sites, such as the *Samuel P. Ely*, *Madeira*, and Split Rock River. Others who helped provide access to dive sites include Stan Braun, who found the *Charlie* anchor; Mike Aeling; and Mike Tougas, who showed me the Split Rock Lighthouse boulder fields. Mike Tougas, Phil Kerber, Bob Karl, and Todd Olson dove the Split Rock Islands in search of the large schooner anchor that is probably from the *Criss Grover*.

Help comes in many different forms. Dave Cooper, currently director of the Voyageurs National Monument in Grand Portage, was instrumental in helping me with the three-dimensional drawing of the *Samuel P. Ely*. He offered suggestions and sketches that helped me work out the appropriate manner in which to portray the splayed sides of the *Ely* at the bow. This was done while we were teaching a Great Lakes Shipwreck Preservation Society (GLSPS) class on underwater documentation and drawing. Jay Cole showed me the Lakewalk dive site, old harbor cribs, and sand and gravel hopper, which I enjoyed and appreciated.

Jeff Redmon, of Redmon Law, the attorney for GLSPS, kindly provided advice to assure the legal aspects of the book were handled in an appropriate manner.

Jerry Eliason graciously loaned me numerous under-

water photographs that he took over the years during his diving exploration of shipwrecks and granted permission to reprint them here.

Elmer Engman granted permission to use several underwater photographs that he had taken while diving different shipwrecks over the years, such as photos of the *Belle P. Cross* rudder and *George Herbert* cargo debris field. Elmer also read the manuscript, offering new information to supplement my findings, such as the *George Herbert* shipwreck debris site.

The late Harold Rochat, of GLSPS, provided useful information about the *Howard*, a shipwreck near Victoria Island; he had written an article about it for the GLSPS newsletter. Several other GLSPS members dove various shipwrecks and verified details in the drawings. My sincere appreciation goes to Bob Anttila, my GLSPS friends and dive buddies, and many others who contributed the use of their images, helped me to research dive sites, or provided details of a shipwreck or other point of interest to explore.

The Minnesota Department of Natural Resources graciously granted permission to use the map depicting the locations of the safe harbors they are developing for boater safety along the North Shore. I appreciate the map of western Lake Superior by *Lake Superior Magazine*, which served as a guide for the map of Lake Superior's North Shore. I also wish to express my appreciation to Richardsons' Marine Publishing and Sportsman's Connection. The *Richardsons' Chartbook and Cruising Guide: Lake Superior* and *Duluth Area Fishing Map Guide* provided good references for drawing the many dive site maps that are included in this book.

Finally, when I thought all was done, my editors, Pam McClanahan of the Minnesota Historical Society Press and Beth Wright of Trio Bookworks, were gracious in helping with suggestions to rewrite sections of the book to appeal to a broader audience. Beth spent considerable time editing the content and providing numerous recommendations to help the nondiver understand what diving shipwrecks is about. Her colleague, Zan Ceeley, in conjunction with the MHS Press staff, did an outstanding job on the layout to provide an interesting format and make the book easy to read. I am very fortunate to have had the support of this group of professionals to make this book possible.

Safe Harbors

Conditions on Lake Superior can change quickly. Divers cruising to dive sites need to check the weather before departing the dock and continue monitoring the sky, seas, and radio to be alert for impending changes. The Minnesota Department of Natural Resources (DNR) is building a series of safe harbors along the North Shore to help boaters get to safety in the event of a storm.

The goal of the DNR is to have a safe harbor within twenty miles of any point along the North Shore up to Canada. Most of the new boat launch sites have been constructed and include docking and mooring sites for a few boats. Improvements will continue to be made to assure boating is safe and convenient for all boaters.

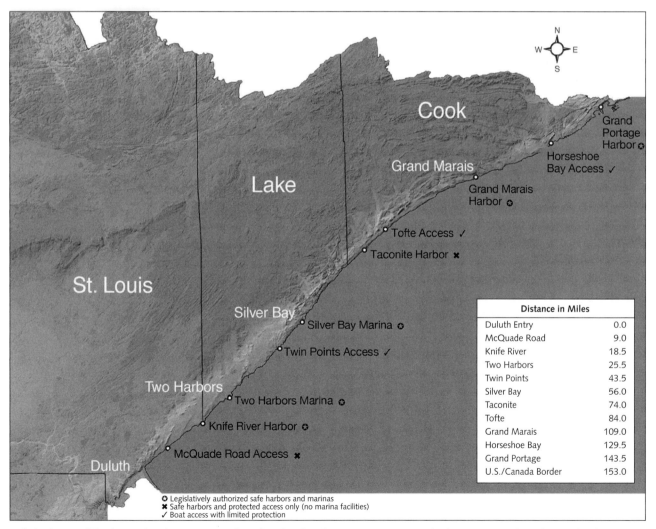

Distance in Miles	
Duluth Entry	0.0
McQuade Road	9.0
Knife River	18.5
Two Harbors	25.5
Twin Points	43.5
Silver Bay	56.0
Taconite	74.0
Tofte	84.0
Grand Marais	109.0
Horseshoe Bay	129.5
Grand Portage	143.5
U.S./Canada Border	153.0

✪ Legislatively authorized safe harbors and marinas
✖ Safe harbors and protected access only (no marina facilities)
✓ Boat access with limited protection

Safe harbors will be located within twenty miles of each other for convenient access by boaters. Boat launches with adequate parking and some type of restroom facilities are available at each location. Courtesy of Minnesota Department of Natural Resources.

SHIPWRECKS
ALONG
LAKE SUPERIOR'S
NORTH SHORE

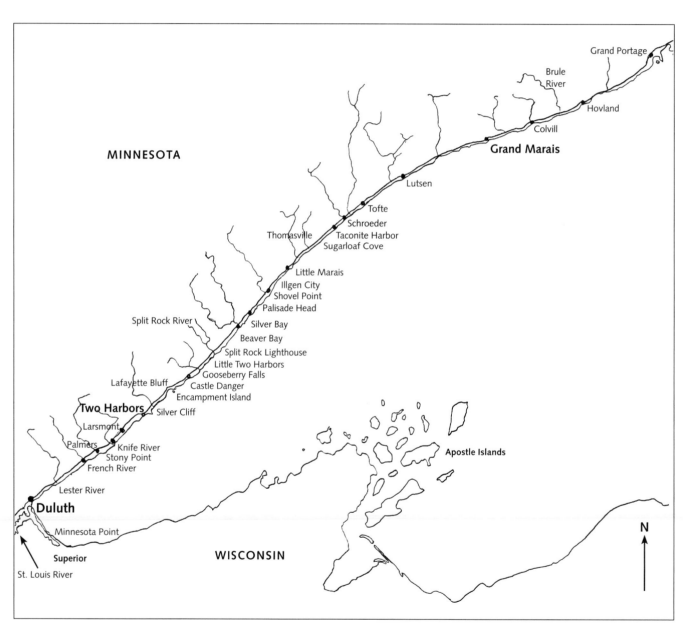

Map 1: **Lake Superior's North Shore.** Drawn by Stephen B. Daniel.

Shipwreck in the St. Louis River at Oliver, Wisconsin

M. C. Neff

The *M. C. Neff* was a 137-foot lumber hooker built at Oshkosh, Wisconsin, and launched in 1888.[1] The 276-ton wooden ship plied Lake Superior waters. In 1909 it hauled lumber up the St. Louis River for construction of the rail and highway bridge at a location just south of Duluth and Oliver, Wisconsin. The wooden ship was anchored in the St. Louis River near the Wisconsin shoreline. A cargo of pilings for the bridge was unloaded September 20, 1909.[2]

THE SINKING

Following the unloading of cargo, the ship caught fire. The *M. C. Neff* burned to the waterline and sank, resulting in a total loss to its owners, Thompson and Lavaque Lumber Company. The crew was able to get off the ship safely, without any loss of life. After the machinery was removed, the ship was left on the bottom of the river.

In the 1960s and 1970s, scuba divers removed artifacts from the sunken ship. Some of these may be viewed in the Fairlawn Mansion, operated by the Superior Public Museums. The mansion is located in Superior, Wisconsin, across from Barker's Island.

THE SHIPWRECK

The frames of the remaining hull bottom section protrude through the murky depth of the river. Debris from the burned ship is inside the hull, which lies parallel to the shore. Ship boards with rusted nails are resting at different angles inside the hull and pose a potential hazard to a diver's drysuit. The planking on the side of the ship facing the shore seems to be intact and curves in near the bottom of the hull. It is estimated that about six feet of the hull sides remain in twelve feet of water. A large wrench may be found in the forward end of the ship, pointed toward Duluth. The windlass is also located in the bow area. The engine lies on its side in the stern at the southerly end of the shipwreck.

Fig. 1: The *M. C. Neff*, as it appeared in use during its lumber hauling days. Courtesy of C. Patrick Labadie Collection, Superior, Wisconsin.

DIVING IS NOT RECOMMENDED

The visibility in the water of the St. Louis River is extremely poor to none, and the current tends to be swift. The water contains tannic acid from decaying foliage in the swamps and lowlands upstream. The result is brackish brown-colored water that is difficult to see through below one foot of depth. Diving this wreck would be a "touching" experience at most.

This shipwreck is best observed by using a depth finder mounted on a boat. Be careful as you approach the site, especially if the water level is low. You risk scraping the bottom of your boat or its propeller on some portions of the ship structure.

The best nearby boat ramp is located around the bend in the river upstream at the Boy Scout Landing on the Minnesota side of the river. The ramp is a city-owned facility and is free, with limited parking.

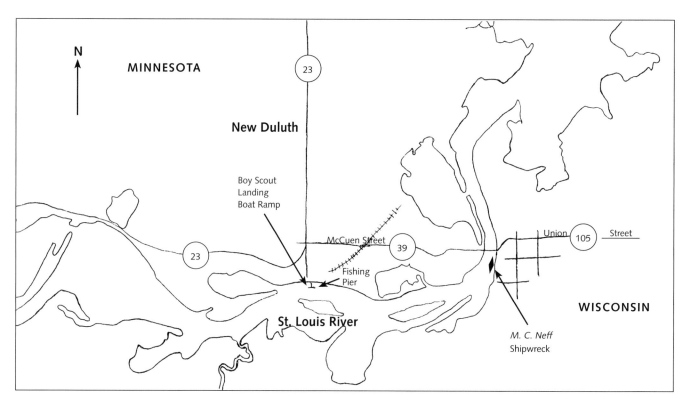

Map 2: Note boat ramp access on the Minnesota side of the St. Louis River. The Oliver Bridge is downriver, east of the boat ramp. Drawn by Stephen B. Daniel.

Fig. 2: The charred wreck of the *M. C. Neff* as it appears on the bottom of the St. Louis River today. Drawing by Stephen B. Daniel.

Fig. 3: The shipwreck lies parallel to shore on the east side of the river, south of the bridge. The charred wreck is about ten feet out from the shore, below the stairs on the hillside. Photo by Stephen B. Daniel.

Shipwrecks in the St. Louis River at Duluth

City of Winnipeg

The *City of Winnipeg* was a package and bulk freight steamer built in Gibraltar, Michigan. It was 184 feet long and grossed 889 tons. This wooden propeller was launched in 1870. Originally called the *Annie L. Craig,*[3] it arrived in Duluth on July 19, 1881, and tied up at the Northern Pacific dock. Stevedores unloaded the ship while the captain and passengers retired for the evening. A fire was discovered near the engine soon afterward.[4] The fire spread quickly on the wooden ship, as the purser and steward hurried to wake passengers and crew. All passengers and most of the crew made it ashore safely. Four of the crew died when the flames cut them off or they drowned trying to escape.

THE SINKING

The burning ship was cut loose to avoid causing damage to the dock and nearby warehouses. It drifted across Superior Bay toward a blast furnace on Minnesota Point. Two tugboats pushed the flaming ship into shallow water, where it burned to the waterline and sank. A portion of the bottom of the ship's hull was all that remained.

THE SHIPWRECK

The burned-out hull was located in the shallow water of Superior Bay, on the west side of Minnesota Point in Duluth. The remaining portion of the *Winnipeg*'s hull was said to have been removed from the shallow water

Fig. 4: The *City of Winnipeg,* a package and bulk freight propeller. Courtesy of Fr. Edward J. Dowling, S.J., Marine Historical Collection, University of Detroit Mercy.

of the harbor sometime after the fire and dragged out to deeper water in Lake Superior. It was then released to settle on the bottom to avoid becoming a navigation hazard. The exact location of the remains of the ship is unknown.

Winslow

The *Winslow* was a 220-foot wooden packet steamer built in Cleveland in 1863.[5] It carried a variety of package cargoes, as well as passengers. The ship caught fire while tied to a dock in the Duluth harbor on October 3, 1891. It had been unloading a cargo of barrels of brown sugar at the St. Paul and Duluth Railroad dock. Only the day before, it had grounded at Lakeside, a neighborhood on the east side of Duluth.

The crew of the *Winslow* noticed a small fire in its wood bunker and tried to extinguish it using standard shipboard procedures—most likely with onboard water buckets, pumps, and firehoses. The fire spread, however, and caused them to call the Duluth fire department. The firefighters found that hoses were too short, and they were unable to reach the ship from hydrants. There were no pumps that could have used the water in the harbor.[6]

THE SINKING

The harbor master ordered the vessel, now engulfed in flames, pushed away from the nearby dock and warehouses. Tugs pushed the burning ship across the bay to the mud flats near Minnesota Point. In spite of efforts by tugboats with fire pumps, the old steamer burned to the waterline. No lives were lost in this incident. The cargo of brown sugar was destroyed in the fire. A brief salvage attempt was made the following year, but the burned hull was determined unfit for rebuilding. The bottom of the ship was later removed upriver to shallow water near the Minnesota Power & Light Company plant (on the west side of the Bong Bridge).

THE SHIPWRECK

Two sections of the shipwreck have been observed using side-scan sonar in the shallow, murky waters by the power plant. About two-thirds of the burned-out hull, along with the propeller and propeller shaft, remain. Some frames may be found, but the water is murky because of the river flow. Some wreckage of the stern may be visible from above when the water level is low.

The poor visibility and shallow water make diving unadvisable. If you visit the site with a small boat, be mindful of protruding structures from the wreck below the surface.

Fig. 5: The *Winslow*, a wooden ship driven by propeller, served Lake Superior for thirty years. Courtesy of Great Lakes Marine Collection, Milwaukee Public Library / Wisconsin Marine Historical Society.

Fig. 6: The *Winslow* burns while docked, in spite of the efforts of tugs to put out the blaze. Courtesy of C. Patrick Labadie Collection, Superior, Wisconsin.

Fig. 7: The wreck of the *Winslow*. Courtesy of Lake Superior Maritime Collection, University of Wisconsin–Superior.

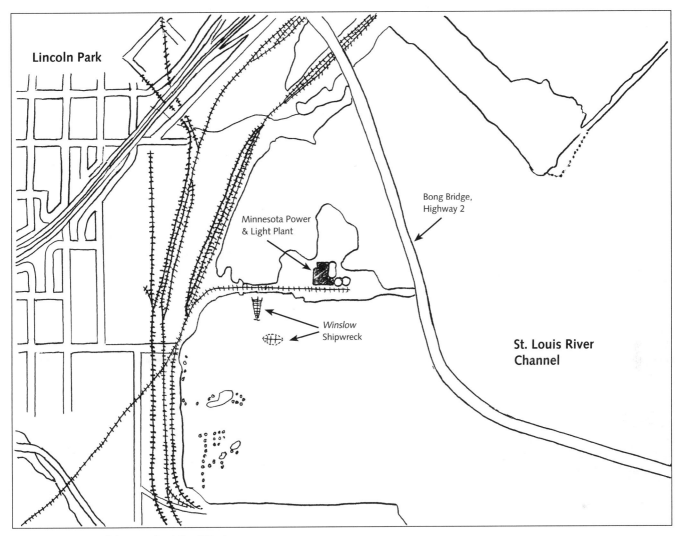

Map 3: Location of the wreck of the *Winslow*.
A boat ramp is located downriver under the
Blatnik Bridge. Drawn by Stephen B. Daniel.

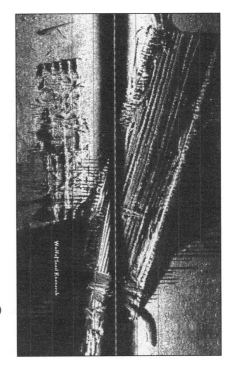

Fig. 8: Side-scan sonar image
of half of the Winslow wreck.
Bottom frames and keelsons
are visible along the bottom of
the bilge. Burned-off futtocks
(where the sides were attached)
protrude along the bottom
edges. Courtesy of Randy Beebe,
Duluth, Minnesota.

Shipwrecks in Lake Superior at Duluth

USS Essex, Minnesota Point

The *USS Essex* was built as a 185-foot war sloop of the enterprise class at the Kittery Navy Yard in East Boston, Massachusetts, in 1874. The ship had a beam of 35 feet and a draft of 14 feet. It was designed by the famous naval architect Donald McKay and was one of eight built as "steam vessels of war with auxiliary sail power."[7] In the mid 1800s McKay designed and built numerous clipper ships that served the commercial trade between the United States and the Far East. The sleek ships were known for their speed, which surpassed that of conventional sailing vessels of the time.

The *Essex* is an example of the combination of steam and sail that would continue into the early part of the next century. The eight ships that included the *USS Essex* were among the last of the sailing vessels designed by McKay. The age of sail and wood-hulled ships was passing, and steam power was fast becoming preferred as the primary means of propulsion for large ships.

Fig. 10: The *USS Essex* on the Maumee River at Toledo, Ohio. Courtesy of Historical Collections of the Great Lakes, Bowling Green State University, Ohio.

The machinery of the *Essex* was built by the Atlantic Works. Commissioned in 1876 and armed, it sailed in both the Atlantic and the Pacific on various Navy assignments until 1893. That year the *Essex* was stationed at Annapolis, Maryland, to provide onboard instruction to naval cadets. It was put out of commission in early 1898, but later that year it was recommissioned to serve as a training ship for apprentice seamen until 1903, when it was again decommissioned by the Navy.

The Ohio Naval Militia acquired the ship in 1904 and used it as a naval militia training vessel at Toledo, Ohio, until 1916. In 1911 the main mast of the *Essex* was removed and installed as the flag staff at Camp Perry near Port Clinton, Ohio. The mast remained in use until it was blown down by a tornado in 1998.

The ship was transferred to Duluth, Minnesota, in 1917 and served as a Minnesota Naval Militia training ship until 1926. It was later converted to floating offices and used by the U.S. Naval Reserve and the Minnesota Naval Militia as a receiving ship in 1928.

THE SCUTTLING

The Navy sold the *Essex* to A. J. Klatzky for $400 on December 23, 1930.[8] Klatzky was president of Klatzky

Fig. 9: Steel engraving of Donald McKay in the McKay Collection, Minnesota Historical Society Collections. Courtesy of Minnesota Historical Society.

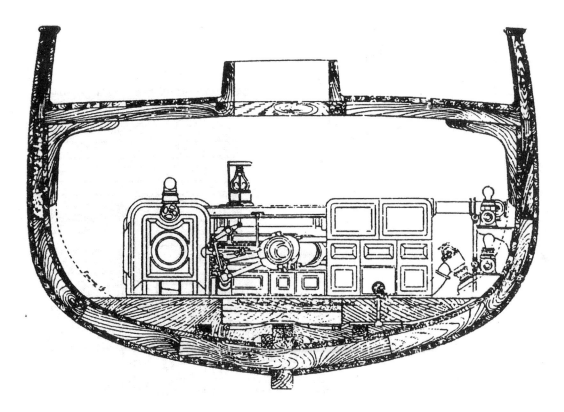

Fig. 11: Cross section showing engine area in an enterprise-class sloop. Drawing by Frank Bennet from *The Steam Navy of the United States* (Westport, CT: Greenwood, 1972). Courtesy of Minnesota Historical Society.

Fig. 12: The *USS Essex* on display for Perry Day celebration in July 1913 at Fairport, Ohio. Note that the main mast has been removed. Courtesy of Historical Collections of the Great Lakes, Bowling Green State University, Ohio.

Fig. 13: Barracks were built over the main deck on the *Essex* during the 1920s. Courtesy of Northeast Minnesota Historical Center.

Iron and Metal Company, a salvage operation. As the ship was scrapped, the salvors removed many pieces of the ship as souvenirs and sent them to former officers and enlisted men who had served on it. Several artifacts removed from the ship were donated to the maritime museum in Canal Park, now the Lake Superior Maritime Visitor Center.

The *Essex* had survived as the oldest steam cruiser in the navy, but it soon passed into history. On October 13, 1931, it was towed out to Lake Superior and moored with heavy steel cables off the northeast end of Minnesota Point, where it was to be scuttled. The next day, it was set ablaze with two hundred gallons of kerosene and oil. The flames burned all night, until the ship was reduced to a smoldering shallow hulk at the edge of the water. The salvors continued to pull the bottom of the hull toward shore as the fire waned. They used a winch on shore to pull the bottom closer to the beach, to prevent it from becoming a navigation hazard.

Today the flat bottom of the hull rests in shallow water near the beach where it was left more than seventy-five years ago. Years of exposure to the elements have further reduced the remains of the ship. People have

Fig. 14: Section of the bottom of the *Essex* by the beach. The keelsons are visible in the center, with the engine bed to the right. Copper rods were used to hold the timbers together. Courtesy of Elmer Engman, Proctor, Minnesota.

Fig. 15: *Essex* wreckage is underwater close to shore. Photo by Stephen B. Daniel.

Fig. 16: Drawing of the *Essex* wreckage as it appears today near the beach at Minnesota Point. Drawing by Tidewater Atlantic Research, courtesy of Minnesota Historical Society.

removed pieces of the wreck for souvenirs or for fires on the beach. This is discouraged today, since the shipwreck is listed on the National Register of Historic Places.

DIVING THE *ESSEX*

Type of Vessel	War sloop
Location	East end of Minnesota Point
GPS Coordinates	46°42.762' N, 92°01.715' W
Depth	2–3 feet
Dive Rating	Not divable; wading only

This wreck site can best be seen by walking along the beach near the end of Minnesota Point. A hiking trail starts near the east side of the Sky Harbor Airport and Seaplane Base; public parking is available outside the airport. The distance from the start of the trail to the wreck site is about 1.75 miles. The *Essex*, which rests in about three feet of water, is about 1,000 feet north of the land-side end of the metal breakwater at the end of Minnesota Point. During storms waves tend to move the sand, so the amount of wreckage visible near the beach may change with time.

Most of the fifty-foot-long bottom section that remains can be seen by wading. Part of the wreck extends from near the sandy beach into the water up to four feet deep. The water leading out into the lake is shallow for quite a distance, so if you're approaching from the lake, beach your boat with caution.

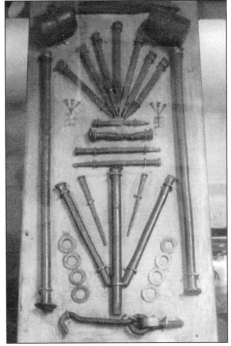

Fig. 17 (above): Detail of engine mount timber at the edge of the beach. Courtesy of Minnesota Historical Society/State Historic Preservation Office.

Fig. 18 (left): Fastenings used on the *Essex* are on display at the *SS Meteor* Whaleback Ship Museum across the harbor on Barker's Island in Superior, Wisconsin. Photo by Stephen B. Daniel.

The *Essex* Mast

When a tornado blew through Camp Perry in 1998, the *Essex* mast, which had been serving as the flagpole, was knocked down; it shattered when it hit the ground. One seven-foot section remained intact. It was discovered afterward that insects had burrowed through the center of the fir mast, weakening its structure.

When the Great Lakes Shipwreck Preservation Society (GLSPS) learned that the remaining section of the mast was temporarily stored at Camp Perry, I met with an administrator, Lt. Col. Ralph Green Jr., there and found that the section was fairly intact and covered with sheet metal. It also sported some bullet holes, since it had been stored briefly near the firing range.

Camp Perry agreed to donate the mast to GLSPS, and Lieutenant Colonel Green also provided several metal pieces from the mast, which had been stored separately. Paul Storch, of the State Preservation Lab, later inspected the mast and provided recommendations on its preservation.

The GLSPS plans to build a historical marker as a tribute to the *Essex* as soon as a suitable location can be found and agreement is reached with a local organization in the Duluth area to install the marker on its property.

Fig 19: The main mast from the *Essex* served as a flagstaff after it was removed from the ship. Courtesy of Anna L. Bovia, Defiance, Ohio.

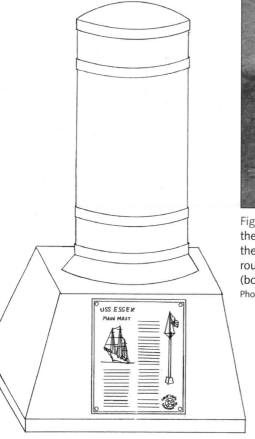

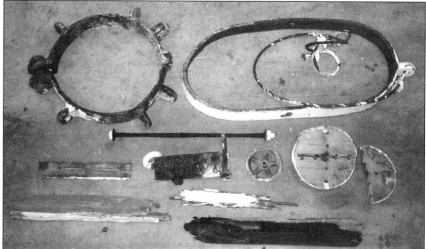

Fig. 20 (above): Donated artifacts included a hand-forged ring that once held the mast stays, an oval hand-forged iron band that once fastened the topmast to the main mast, a brass pulley, a curved brass plate, a two-foot-long bolt, and the rounded mast tip, held together with wooden dowels. Pieces of the wooden mast (bottom of photo) show the fine fir grain, as well as insect and dry rot damage. Photo by Stephen B. Daniel.

Fig. 21 (left): *Essex* Historical Marker: The GLSPS developed a steel supporting structure for the mast section based on the recommendation of a member who is a structural engineer. The base will stand on a concrete pad. The wood of the mast will be restored and covered with metal (as it is currently). The two iron bands will be reinstalled, along with a cleat. A cap will be fabricated to protect the top end of the mast from the elements.
A collar will be constructed to extend around the lower end of the mast section. Seals will also be used to protect it. Drawing by Stephen B. Daniel.

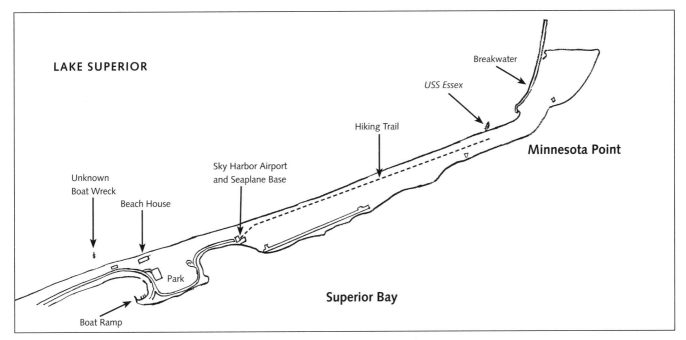

Map 4: Minnesota Point: the locations of the *Essex* and the unknown boat wreck. Drawn by Stephen B. Daniel.

Unknown Boat Wreck at Minnesota Point

Type of Vessel	Tugboat
Location	Minnesota Point, 450 feet offshore and 500 feet northwest of beach house
Depth	Approximately 4 feet
Dive Rating	Novice diver

A second wreck can be found farther west of the *Essex* wreck site. It is an unknown boat, perhaps the remains of an old tug. A chart at Minnesota Point shows that the wreck is in about 4 feet of water (depth may vary) approximately 450 feet from shore.[9] The wreck site is about 500 feet northwest of the beach house in the park at Minnesota Point.

Diving the Unknown Wreck at Minnesota Point

The bottom of the forty-foot vessel may be observed. Snorkeling may be sufficient to investigate this shipwreck, and the best dive would be from a boat. However, if you attempt a shore dive, you will need to enter the beach through the beach house at the park. (The beach is surrounded by private property.) Parking is available in the park. You will have to pay a small admission fee to enter the beach house and gain access to the beach.

Amethyst, Minnesota Point

On February 18, 2007, a small piece of wreckage was found south of the Lift Bridge, about 150 yards offshore from the 2600 block at Minnesota Point.[10] Isaac Ginsberg, John Williams, Steve Sola, and his daughter Sophie were skating on clear ice on Lake Superior behind their homes when they discovered the wreckage. It was in about ten feet of water and could be seen through the ice. They returned to shore to obtain their ice-fishing auger and fishing drop camera. After drilling a small hole in the ice, they lowered the camera to view the wreckage. Their find was unique, so they reported it to Thom Holden at the Lake Superior Maritime Visitor Center on Park Point. Since the vessel was at this point unknown, Thom decided to call it the *SS Sophie* after the little girl who was very excited about seeing her first shipwreck.

The Great Lakes Shipwreck Preservation Society (GLSPS) was contacted to explore the wreckage under the ice and help identify the vessel. Divers from GLSPS on safety tether lines descended through a large hole cut in the ice to examine and document the wreckage. They measured it and photographed it with a still camera and video.

The documentation helped determine that the wreckage was too small to be the tug *Inman*, an eighty-one-foot tugboat that was junked and burned in 1916, sinking to the sandy bottom off Minnesota Point. Some large pieces of that wreckage were reported in 1986 to have been uncovered in the sand closer to the south pier

Fig. 22: *Amethyst.* Drawing by Stephen B. Daniel.

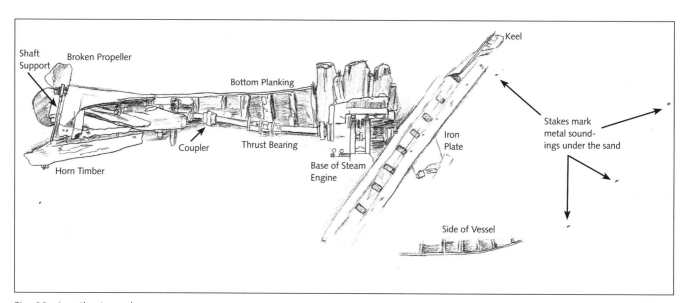

Fig. 23: *Amethyst* wreckage. Drawing by Stephen B. Daniel.

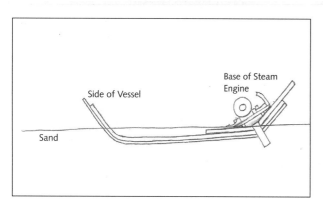

Fig. 24: Cross section of *Amethyst* wreckage, which is partially buried in sand. Drawing by Stephen B. Daniel.

Fig. 25: The base of the small steam engine is secured to some bottom boards. Two flywheels are still attached to the prop shaft. Courtesy of Ken Merryman, Fridley, Minnesota.

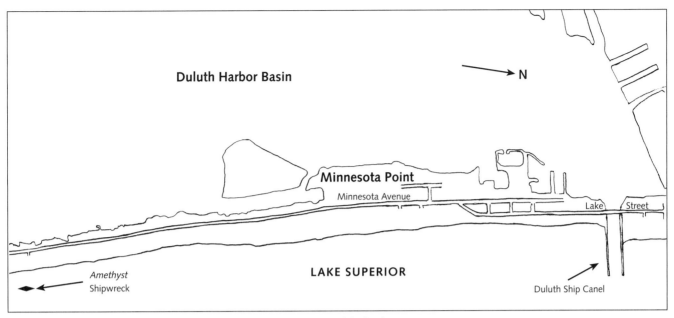

Map 5: The *Amethyst* is located 150 yards offshore from the 2600 block of Minnesota Point. Drawn by Stephen B. Daniel.

of the Duluth Ship Canal. Other candidates were the *Sara Smith*, a sixty-five-foot tugboat that burned and sank off Minnesota Point, and the *Amethyst*, a forty-five-foot tug that had been scuttled off Minnesota Point.

The small wreckage measured 33.5 feet from the propeller (52 inches in diameter) to the forward section. The overall length from the propeller hub to the point where the shaft extended out of the base of the small steam engine was 21 feet, 1 inch. The outside piece of hull measured 7.5 feet from the keel; the bottom of the beam was estimated to be 15 feet. The base of the engine block measured about 3 feet. The documenting crew was puzzled by two hollow counterweights attached to the crankshaft below the engine base, since a large tugboat would usually have much heavier, solid counterweights. The drive shaft measured 1 foot in circumference, which translates to a 3.8-inch shaft coming out of the engine.[11] The planking under the engine base was 2 inches thick, while the bottom planks under the propeller shaft were 1.5 inches thick.

The size of the planking, engine, and structural wreckage would indicate that the remains were from a smaller vessel, such as the forty-five-foot *Amethyst*. After comparing a drawing of the wreckage to a photo of the *Amethyst* from Historical Collections of the Great Lakes at Bowling Green State University, Ohio, the GLSPS team concluded that the vessel must be the *Amethyst*. The *Amethyst* was a fourteen-ton tug that worked many years in the harbors around Duluth and Superior, as well as along the North Shore of Minnesota. It was involved in rescuing the crew of the tug *Siskiwit* when it hit a reef near Grand Marais in 1879.

DIVING THE *AMETHYST*

Type of Vessel	Tugboat
Location	150 yards offshore from 2600 block, Minnesota Point
GPS Coordinates	46°45.461' N, 92°04.411' W
Depth	7 feet
Dive Rating	Novice diver

The *Amethyst* wreckage consists of the keel section, midship to stern. The broken propeller, shaft with coupler, and lower engine structure are visible, depending on sand movement caused by stormy seas.

Fig. 26: A diver scans the sandy bottom with his underwater metal detector. Another diver follows his lead and presses plastic stakes in the sand to mark metal readings. The shadow above is the ice on top of the lake. Courtesy of Ken Merryman, Fridley, Minnesota.

Guido Pfister, Duluth Ship Canal, South Pier

The *Guido Pfister* was a wooden merchant schooner built in 1873. The ship was 198 feet in length and grossed 691 tons.[12]

THE SINKING

The ship was involved in an accident on October 10, 1885, as it approached the old Duluth Ship Canal where a tug waited to take it through.[13] A towline was tossed to a crewman aboard the tug so that the *Pfister* could be towed through the Ship Canal. The crewman missed the towline, and the schooner kept gliding toward the south pier. It struck hard on the rocks of the pier. While the crew jumped safely to shore, the rocks ripped the bottom out of the ship, making it a total loss.

Captain Alexander McDougal, a Duluth native, salvaged much of the coal cargo. Some local residents on Minnesota Point also acquired some of the coal. The ship was abandoned, and the hull was left to rot in place. Most of the hull was removed in 1898, before the Duluth harbor entry was reconstructed.

During major rehabilitation of the south pier, between 1985 and 1987, the U.S. Army Corps of Engineers recovered portions of the hull and some coal from the *Pfister*. Some of these items are now in a collection at the Lake Superior Maritime Visitor Center.

Since the ship was mostly removed during two different periods of reconstruction of the south pier of the Duluth Ship Canal, not much of its hull can be expected to remain. Nevertheless, some divers claim to have seen debris near the cribbing. Although access by boat may be possible, diving this shipwreck site is not recommended.

Mataafa, Duluth Entry

The *Mataafa* was a 430-foot steamer grossing 4,840 tons. It was launched in Lorain, Ohio, under the name *Pennsylvania* in 1899.[14] On November 27, 1905, the *Mataafa* departed Duluth towing the 366-foot, 3,422-ton barge *James Naysmyth* as its consort. They were off of Two Harbors in the early evening when a terrible gale hit them. They struggled against heavy seas but could not make any headway for nearly ten hours. The captain of the *Mataafa* decided to turn around and head back to Duluth. There

Fig. 27: The *Mataafa* after striking the Duluth Ship Canal North Pier a second time. Fig. 28 (inset): Wind and waves push the *Mataafa* into the north pier. Both images courtesy of Kenneth E. Thro Collection, Lake Superior Maritime Collection, University of Wisconsin–Superior.

was no way they could make it towing the barge, so the *Naysmyth* was left anchored about two miles offshore from the entry to the Duluth harbor. The barge survived the storm intact, avoiding the fate of the steamer.

As the *Mataafa* made a run for the Duluth Ship Canal, an enormous wave picked it up, forcing its bow into the sandy bottom and slamming the ship into the north pier head.[15] The ship was hit by more waves, turning it perpendicular to the pier. The ship still had power but was immobilized; the rudder had been sheared off when the ship struck the pier.[16] Huge waves washed over the ship, putting out the fire in the boiler and causing its engine to quit. The *Mataafa* was then left helpless in the storm. Another huge sea lifted the ship up and turned it around, leaving it aground in shallower water about six hundred feet from shore and a hundred feet from the north pier.

THE SINKING

The intense storm continued to beat on the ship, causing it to break apart amidships. The ship settled to the bottom as the storm raged on. The twenty-four-man crew was separated, with half of the men on the bow and half on the stern. Three crewmen were able to make a quick run for the bow, while nine men were forced to remain in the stern section. The loss of engine power meant there would be no heat in the stern. The nine men

Fig. 29: The beached *Mataafa* with heavy seas sweeping over its decks. Courtesy of Kenneth E. Thro Collection, Lake Superior Maritime Collection, University of Wisconsin–Superior.

in the stern section perished of exposure, as temperatures hovered near zero with gale winds in excess of sixty miles an hour.

Lifesavers rushed to Duluth on a tugboat, after rescuing the crew of the steamer *England*, which had been pushed aground by the storm about 2.5 miles south of the Duluth Canal, north of the Oatka Recreation Center. The rough seas made it impossible for the *Mataafa* crew to see or catch any of the lifelines that were tossed toward the stranded ship. The lifesaving crew was forced to wait until the weather subsided before making another attempt. Meanwhile, about ten thousand people from Duluth gathered around bonfires on shore in the dark freezing weather to watch the terrible scenario taking place so close in front of them.

Fig. 30: The *Mataafa* shipwreck after the storm, northwest of the Duluth Ship Canal piers. Courtesy of Northeast Minnesota Historical Center.

The men in the bow gathered up lamps, wooden furniture, and wood paneling. They then dragged a bathtub into the windlass room, where the captain started a fire to keep them from freezing during the night. At daybreak, the lifesavers launched their surfboat in the still dangerous waters and were able to reach the ship. They quickly evacuated the fifteen surviving crewmen.

The captain had worked his way to the stern before leaving the ship, finding four dead crewmen frozen on the icy top deck. The others were missing, presumed to be washed overboard.

SALVAGE AND A RENEWED LIFE ON THE LAKES

The *Mataafa* was refloated six months later and removed by Reids of Sarnia.[17] It was rebuilt at a cost of over $100,000 and returned to service. It went on to sail the Great Lakes as an ore freighter and was converted to an automobile carrier in 1948,[18] continuing to sail in this capacity in 1950 and 1951. The *Mataafa* was retired along with numerous other smaller Great Lakes vessels when the locks and channels of the St. Lawrence Seaway were enlarged.[19]

The *Mataafa* steamed out of port for the last time on October 23, 1964. It sailed through the St. Lawrence Seaway under its own power and was taken to Hamburg, Germany, where it was dismantled for scrap.

Diving is not recommended: since the ship was salvaged, there is no shipwreck to see.

Fig. 31: The *Mataafa* was an automobile carrier until its retirement in 1964. Courtesy of Lake Superior Maritime Collection, University of Wisconsin–Superior.

Historic Artifacts in Lake Superior at Duluth

Sand and Gravel Hopper, Downtown Lakewalk

The sand and gravel hopper is referred to locally as "Uncle Harvey's Mausoleum"[20] and as "Cribs" on navigational charts. The hopper is located near the Lakewalk behind a hotel. This structure was built by the Whitney brothers of Superior, Wisconsin, during the winter of 1919. It was abandoned in 1922 because of problems with intense and unpredictable weather.

Harvey Whitney conceived the idea of building the sand and gravel hopper on the lake side of Canal Park to avoid the delay of ships waiting to pass through the ship canal. He needed the hopper to improve the method of unloading sand and gravel offshore for his business. The city of Duluth had tried to build an outer harbor in 1872. Harvey thought it might still build one, which would protect his investment in the structure.

Ships brought sand to Duluth that had been removed from the lake around the Apostle Islands. Gravel was also mined in Grand Marais and transported to Duluth by ship. The steam tug *William A. Whitney* towed the scow *Limit*, after it had been filled with sand, across the lake to Duluth. The scow was tied to the side of the hopper's concrete foundation, where the bollards can be seen today. Two steam-powered clam shells were used to unload the scow and transfer the sand or gravel to the steel hopper inside the concrete building. The hopper emptied the sand or gravel onto a large conveyor belt that operated on a trestle. The sand and gravel were carried to shore, where they were emptied into the top of a tunnel. Trucks positioned themselves in the tunnel to receive the sand and gravel as it dropped off the conveyor belt.

DEMISE OF THE SAND AND GRAVEL HOPPER

The city of Duluth never built an outer harbor. Fierce storms took a toll on the concrete structure of the hopper. Weather would make it difficult for ships to dock, since the hopper was so exposed on the lake.

Fig. 32: The sand and gravel hopper with conveyor system in place, April 1920. Photo by Hugh McKenzie courtesy of Kenneth E. Thro Collection, Lake Superior Maritime Collection, University of Wisconsin–Superior.

Fig. 33: The sand and gravel hopper today, near the Lakewalk in Canal Park. Photo by Stephen B. Daniel.

Whitney was forced to discontinue use of the hopper in 1922, after only three years of operation. The structure was left to the elements.

The steel trestle carrying the conveyor belt was probably the first thing to fall away. The concrete pylons that supported it at the base are still intact, though quite weathered for their age. The hopper lost its roof many years ago. The cribbing supporting the structure has settled into the sand, probably as a result of erosion near the base during many strong storms. The concrete structure is still mostly above the surface of the water, although the deck is submerged, except for the northeast corner and

outer east side. The steel hopper may be observed inside. The pointed design of the northeast end of the building has helped preserve the structure by breaking heavy seas. Ice has caused additional damage, resulting in pieces of concrete falling away from areas touching the water.

DIVING THE SAND AND GRAVEL HOPPER

Location	Duluth waterfront, offshore from the rocky shore along the Lakewalk at Canal Park
Depth	14 feet
Dive Rating	Novice diver

Boats may be launched at a public ramp under the Blatnik Bridge. A short cruise through the ship canal and around the north pier will place you near the hopper.

Shore access is also possible. You can park in the parking lot next to Endion Station. For a shore dive, enter at the beach, and swim south to the cement pylon structure just off shore. View it underwater; then swim to the sand and gravel hopper, entering it underwater.

Divers may swim to the structures in the water on calm days without difficulty, but boat access may be

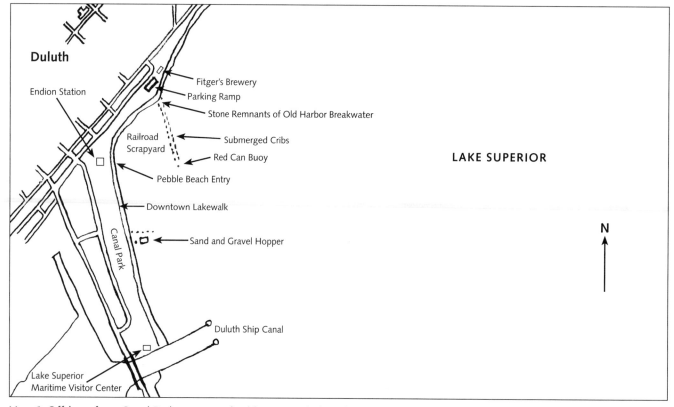

Map 6: Offshore from Canal Park are many divable sites, including the sand and gravel hopper, railroad scrapyard (see pp. 21–23), and old harbor breakwater cribs (see pp. 23–25). Drawn by Stephen B. Daniel.

Fig. 34: Cutaway of sand and gravel hopper showing the steel beams anchored to the concrete sides. Cribbing is visible underwater, below the concrete deck. *Drawing by Stephen B. Daniel.*

Fig. 35: Cement pylon located behind the hopper. Steel plates are bolted to the cement and pilings inside the structure. *Drawing by Stephen B. Daniel.*

Fig. 36 (below, right): Site of the railroad scrapyard near the Lakewalk in Canal Park. The Lakewalk along the shore on the north side was built over the old wharf. *Photo by Stephen B. Daniel.*

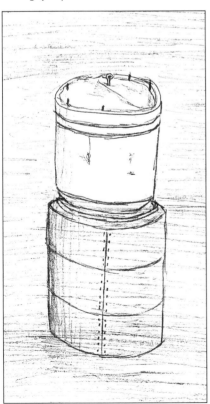

the best way to visit this site. Anchoring securely to the sandy bottom is recommended, as the cement structure's sides are very rough.

Divers may find it interesting to swim around the outside of the structure first. Entry is best achieved lakeside. You can swim through gaps in the bottom of the structure. Most of the inside can be reached by swimming. Some areas can be reached by climbing out of the water onto the cement floor. Use caution—the algae-covered cement may be slippery.

Railroad Scrapyard, Downtown Lakewalk

The north section of the downtown Lakewalk was built over an old wharf. Remnants of the wharf can still be seen underwater, near the edge of the walk. A railroad operated near London Road on the hill above the Lakewalk. Trains carried passengers to points along the North Shore for many years in the first half of the twentieth century.

A rail repair yard was located near the shore of Lake Superior, not far from what is a parking ramp today. Many parts that were broken or no longer needed were thrown into the lake nearby, which served as an underwater junkyard. This site has been referred to as "Caryn's Scrapyard," probably named for one of the operators.

Endion Station was moved to its current site in Canal Park in 1986, when Interstate Highway 35 was routed through the city. The original location of this

Fig. 37: Endion Station with the D&IR No. 46 engine in front, its cars loaded with logs. Courtesy of Frank King Collection.

Fig. 38: Endion Station as it appears today. Photo by Stephen B. Daniel.

train station was to the east, on the waterfront at 1504 South Street, below London Road.[21]

Passengers first used the train station after the sandstone building was constructed in 1899. Passenger service continued for sixty-two years. In addition to riding to downtown Duluth for work, passengers used the train to travel to towns along the North Shore and up to Ely for recreation.

Daily passenger service ended in 1961, and Endion

Station was used for transporting freight until it was closed in 1978. Endion Station at one point housed the offices of the Duluth Convention and Visitors Bureau and currently is occupied by a store and a Duluth Police Department substation. The old rail line is now referred to as the Lake Shore Line. Excursion trains, operating from the depot in downtown Duluth, carry passengers to the Glensheen Mansion and further up the shore to Two Harbors.

DIVING THE RAILROAD SCRAPYARD

Location	About 100 feet offshore from pebble beach in front of northwest Lakewalk at Canal Park
Depth	16 feet
Dive Rating	Novice diver

This dive may be done from either shore or a boat. There are two possibilities for parking. One is the parking lot near Endion Station, which is closest to the beach. You may also use the public parking ramp accessible from Superior Street (see map 6, p. 20).

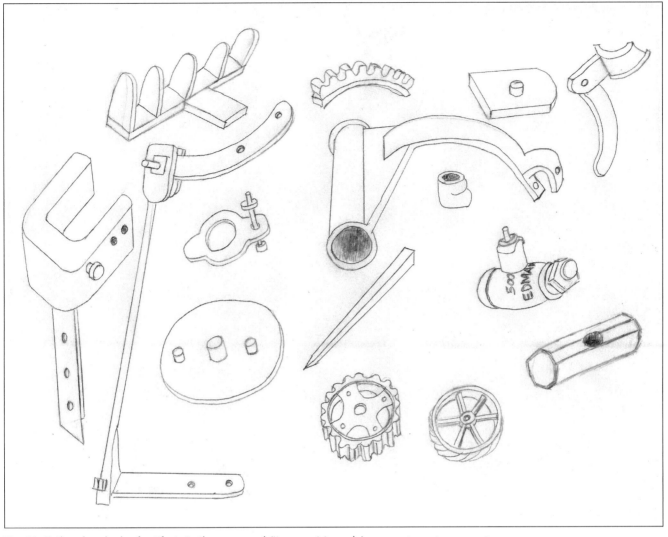

Fig. 39: Railroad and wharf artifacts in the scrapyard (items not to scale). Drawing by Stephen B. Daniel.

If you prefer to enter from shore, it is best to use the pebble beach area next to Canal Park. Do not use the Lakewalk for entry near the ramp, since you could obstruct the walk and the drop to the water makes exiting extremely difficult, if not impossible.

Divers may enter the water from the beach and swim toward the corner and along the north side where the old wharf can be seen underwater. If you dive from a boat, anchor offshore to avoid hooking or damaging artifacts. The railroad scrapyard is an easy swim from a boat on a calm day.

Many train artifacts are located on the sandy bottom along the north side of the old wharf, slightly out from shore. Water depth in the artifact area is about sixteen feet. Many parts on the bottom appear to be from locomotives, including wheels, gears, brass valves, pipes, and connecting shafts and bars. There are also what appear to be a variety of interesting steel implements

resting on the sand. Divers will also notice rails scattered about.

Enjoy observing the many unusual items, but remember that these scrap pieces are now artifacts and belong to the State of Minnesota. They must remain underwater where you find them. This practice will assure that there will be much for other divers to see as well.

Old Harbor Breakwater Cribs, Downtown Lakewalk

When Alexander McDougal was forced to unload passengers and cargo from his ship by using a large rock outcropping near shore, it was clear a harbor was needed.[22] In the early 1870s, the Superior and Mississippi Railroad arrived in Duluth. A breakwater, dock, and grain

Fig. 40: Stone ruins of the old harbor breakwater on shore by the Lakewalk. The Vietnam Veterans Memorial is nearby. The cribs extend out at an angle from this point on shore. Photo by Stephen B. Daniel.

Fig. 41: The Blatnik Bridge serves as an excellent landmark for the Rice's Point Boat Launch site. The launch, which has adequate parking, is located under the bridge. Photo by Stephen B. Daniel.

elevator were built a little west of where the Fitger's Brewery building stands today (see map 6, p. 20). Ships used this harbor until the Duluth Ship Canal was dug across Park Point to connect Lake Superior to the inner harbor. The old harbor was abandoned afterward and gradually deteriorated from years of exposure to the elements.

The breakwater was built out from shore near the point of land now used for the Vietnam Veterans Memorial on the shoreline near the Lakewalk. Stacked stones at the edge of the shore mark the point where the breakwater began, extending out into Lake Superior for about two hundred feet. The breakwater was part of the old harbor. It was built on a series of cribs that rose from the bottom of the lake and extended out from shore. Square timbers were notched and linked together to form the sides of the cribs. Planks were fastened to the timbers to form a bottom.

The cribs were probably then floated out from shore and filled with rocks to weight them for sinking. The

rocks also helped secure the cribs to the sandy bottom of the lake. The breakwater was actually a double row of cribbing, which may be observed underwater. Timbers and planking were built over the top of the cribs to construct a wide dock that could accommodate trucks or other vehicles. Ships would sail to the protected (southwest) side of the breakwater to tie up. Goods would then be unloaded from the ships and transported to commercial places, such as the brewery.

The breakwater often took a beating from storms and ice as the seasons changed. This weather action eventually destroyed the breakwater that was above the surface of the water. Today the cribs are all that remain of the old breakwater. These are marked on navigation charts and may easily be reached by boat. There is a second short row of cribs on the lake side of the old breakwater crib. This may have been a dock that was constructed alongside the breakwater. It is best to locate the cribs on a depth finder before dropping anchor outside, to avoid potential damage to the structure below the surface. The cribs are located at a twenty-two-foot depth.

The cribs now serve as a spawning ground for lake trout. You may see fish swimming around and through the cribs. This site is a protected area for lake trout spawning, so fishing is prohibited. But the fish do make this an interesting dive site.

ACCESS TO THE OLD HARBOR BREAKWATER CRIBS

For shore divers, public parking is available in a ramp off Superior Street. Head toward the Vietnam Veterans Memorial by the Lakewalk. The shore entry point for the cribs is near the stone remnants at the water's edge. Divers may find the cribs a short distance from shore, heading toward the north pier of the Duluth Ship Canal.

If you plan on a boat dive, the Rice's Point Boat Launch is one of the most convenient in the area. Located under the Blatnik Bridge, it is a free launch site close to the Duluth Harbor Basin. The launch may be reached by taking I-35 to the I-535/US 53 route heading east toward the bridge. Take the first exit before the bridge to Garfield Avenue.

A sign under the bridge marks the Rice's Point Boat Launch. Two ramp areas are available. The best ramp is on the east side, near a fishing pier. The ramp is provided and maintained by cooperation of the City of Duluth, the Seaway Port Authority, the Minnesota Department of Transportation, and the Minnesota Power Company. Small docks are located along the ramps for convenient boarding. Vehicles and boat trailers may be parked in the lot under the bridge.

The Duluth waterfront may be reached by a short cruise through the Duluth Harbor Basin and the Duluth Ship Canal. This boat launch also offers access to shipwrecks off Minnesota Point (see pp. 8–15). A cruise through Superior Bay and Superior Harbor Basin will lead out through the Wisconsin Entry.

Diving the Old Harbor Breakwater Cribs

Location	About 50 feet offshore from the stone remnants by the Lakewalk near the Vietnam Veterans Memorial
Depth	22 feet
Dive Rating	Novice diver

Divers may enter from shore, starting out from the stone remnants at a slight angle in the direction of the ship canal's north pier. The cribs extend from the stone remnants on shore out into the lake to just short of the red can buoy at the lake end. Visibility may be about fifteen feet, depending on the weather. The double section of cribs consists of a twenty-four-foot span constructed of two twelve-foot pieces. A gap occurs in the cribs near the lake end. The red can buoy is just beyond this section. The depth is about twenty-two feet.

In addition to the crib structure and fish, some discarded items may be seen on the bottom of the lake.

Among these are railroad rails, square steel rods, and an iron grid piece. The cribs make for a long swim and offer a lot of structure to see. The number of fish will depend on the time of year. This site is also an excellent night dive, when more marine life is active.

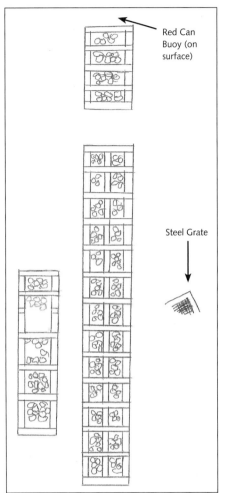

Fig. 42 (left): Two rows of cribs may be observed underwater. Drawing by Stephen B. Daniel.

Fig. 43 (below): The old harbor breakwater was built on cribs; (inset) steel rails and bars nearby. Drawing by Stephen B. Daniel.

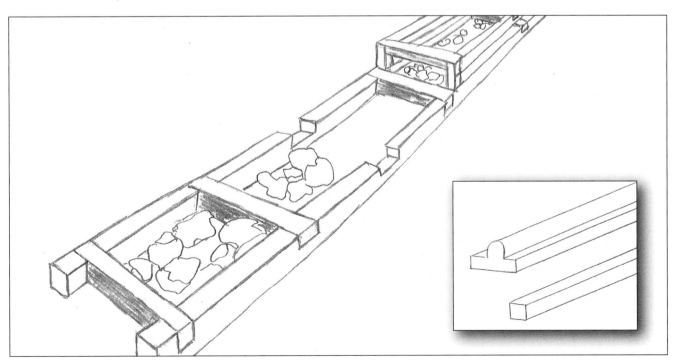

Shipwrecks in Lake Superior at Duluth

PART 2

Thomas Wilson, Duluth Entry

The *Thomas Wilson* was a whaleback: a ship whose round hull had blunt points on both ends. Captain Alexander McDougal began to design and build whalebacks in Duluth in 1888. The shipyard operations were moved across the harbor to Superior, Wisconsin, after only six ships had been built, when the City of Duluth declared that no shipyards could be located within its limits.

The whaleback's design was streamlined; its rounded sides allowed seas to drain away from the deck easily. Turrets were constructed at the bow and stern to house gear and crew and provide access to areas of the ship below deck. Officers' quarters, galley, mess hall, and pilothouse were typically housed in the cabin structure above the stern turrets. Several versions of whalebacks were built. Some were barges; many were bulk carriers; and one, the *Christopher Columbus*, was a passenger steamer.

Fig. 44: Captain Alexander McDougal held many patents, including the single-fluke anchor his whalebacks carried. Courtesy of Lake Superior Maritime Collection, University of Wisconsin–Superior.

Fig. 45: A group of VIPs crowds the bow of the *Wilson*, here showing its unique curved hull. Courtesy of Kenneth E. Thro Collection, Lake Superior Maritime Collection, University of Wisconsin–Superior.

Fig. 46: Drawing of the *Thomas Wilson* by Ken Tunnel. Courtesy of Stewart Taylor Printing, Duluth, Minnesota.

Fig. 47: The *Wilson*'s triangular anchor on the portside bow and large kedge starboard anchor distinguished the whaleback from other ships. In the background, a consort barge waits with the *Wilson* to enter the locks. Courtesy of Kenneth E. Thro Collection, Lake Superior Maritime Collection, University of Wisconsin–Superior.

The *Thomas Wilson*'s keel was laid on November 7, 1891, in the Superior Shipyard. The ship was launched on April 30, 1892, as hull number 119. It was 308 feet in length, with a beam of 38 feet and a depth of 24 feet. The bulk steamer was powered by a triple-expansion steam engine. The ship was named after a friend and financial backer of Alexander McDougal who owned and operated the Wilson Steamship Line.[23]

The *Wilson* started its life on the lakes hauling wheat from the Twin Ports to ports out east and returned with loads of coal. It changed owners a few times, ending up in the fleet of the Pittsburgh Steamship Company in 1901. Iron ore was now the cargo, one that it carried on its last voyage from the Twin Ports.

The Sinking

The lake was calm on June 7, 1902, when the *Wilson* left the Duluth Ship Canal fully loaded and moving slowly. The *George G. Hadley*, a wooden steamer loaded with coal, was inbound, headed toward the canal. The tug *Annie L. Smith* was dispatched to inform the captain of the *Hadley* to change course and proceed to the Superior Entry. By the time the news was received on board the *Hadley*, it was already dangerously close to the *Wilson*.

Not looking in the direction of the *Wilson*, the *Hadley*'s Captain Fitzgerald ordered the wheelsman to turn the steamer to port, which headed the ship directly

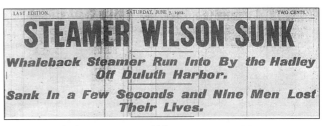

Fig. 48: *Duluth Evening Herald* from June 7, 1902.

toward the *Wilson*. Regardless of what the wheelsman might observe or think should be done, the captain's orders had to be followed. Moments later, the *Hadley* rammed the hull of the *Wilson* just forward of the rear-most hatch, ripping a deep gash in the side of the whaleback.

The hatch covers of the *Wilson* had not been placed in position, leaving the cargo hold hatches open to the waters of Lake Superior, which rushed in when the ship lurched during the collision. The whaleback sank in about three minutes, leaving little time for the crew to escape. Nine men perished in the stern of the ship as it sank bow first. The iron ship settled upright on the bottom as the *Hadley* steamed toward the beach at Minnesota Point, alongside the Duluth Ship Canal.[24]

Then the *Hadley* also settled in the water, but the bow, the top of the rear cabin, and the stacks protruded from the shallow depth. The *Hadley* was raised and removed at the salvage cost of half its value, while the *Wilson* was declared a total loss. There have been three

Fig. 49: The *George G. Hadley* with its twin stacks. Courtesy of Kenneth E. Thro Collection, Lake Superior Maritime Collection, University of Wisconsin–Superior.

Fig. 50 (below): The wrecking of the *Thomas Wilson* by Kurt Carlson. Courtesy of Great Lakes Shipwreck Museum, Whitefish Point, Michigan.

attempts to salvage the *Wilson*: the first in 1902; then in 1939, when the Wieland brothers purchased the whaleback but abandoned the ship after completing one dive; and the last in 1962. All failed.[25]

The *Wilson* lay on the bottom undisturbed until the 1960s, when scuba diving equipment became available to allow sport divers to visit the shipwreck. According to Elmer Engman, "The *Wilson* hides many secrets and if you are not careful, you will pass them by."[26] While diving the wrecked whaleback in 1972, he discovered one of the bow anchors. The anchor was lying alongside the bow on the starboard side of the ship. Following the iron stock to the sand, Elmer found the flukes and concluded it was the starboard anchor. He later helped the Coast Guard raise the anchor to the surface. It is displayed by the Duluth Lakewalk in Canal Park. The McDougal patent anchor, which was once secured on the port side of the *Wilson*'s bow, was also retrieved and is displayed nearby.

Fig. 51 (right): The *Wilson*'s spar extended above the surface after sinking. Courtesy of Robert R. Abernathy Collection, University of Wisconsin–Superior.

Fig. 52 (below): The tug *Annie L. Smith* approaches the sinking *Hadley*. Courtesy of Kenneth E. Thro Collection, Lake Superior Maritime Collection, University of Wisconsin–Superior.

Fig. 53: The *Hadley* was considered salvageable, even with its bow stuck in the sand. Courtesy of Kenneth E. Thro Collection, Lake Superior Maritime Collection, University of Wisconsin–Superior.

Fig. 54: The *Wilson*'s stern rose high in the air as it sank, according to witnesses. Photo of watercolor by June W. Perry courtesy of Lake Superior Maritime Collection, University of Wisconsin–Superior.

THE SHIPWRECK

The *Wilson* is partially buried in the sandy bottom in about seventy feet of water, about a mile out from the Duluth Ship Canal. The sand comes up to about a foot below its fantail. The rusty hull is broken in several areas. The break nearest the stern on the port side is the site of the collision that caused the ship to sink. Several other breaks in the hull are probably due to anchors being dropped on it over the years while vessels were waiting for dockage in the harbor.

The bow of the hull points toward the east; it is quite well preserved, displaying intact bollards and fairleads.

Fig. 55: The USCGC *Sundew* raises the *Wilson*'s starboard folding stock anchor, which is later restored and displayed in Canal Park. Photo by Nordic Underwater Enterprises, courtesy of Lake Superior Maritime Collection, University of Wisconsin–Superior.

Fig. 56: The one-and-a-half-ton Trotman folding stock anchor from the *Thomas Wilson*, on display along the Lakewalk. The Duluth Lift Bridge and the Lake Superior Maritime Visitor Center are visible in the background. Photo by Stephen B. Daniel.

The triple mooring eye on the nose is of special interest. The anchor windlass is located inside the forward turret. Warping heads that were once used for the dock lines extend out each side of the turret. The hull in the bow area is intact up to the second cargo hatch opening.

The upper structure of the rear turrets was removed as a navigation hazard after the sinking. The three lower sections of the rear turrets are visible, covered with a single deck surface. The top of the engine may be observed by peering through the middle turret, which was above the engine room. Some bollards and a broken capstan may be observed at the rear of the ship.

DIVING THE *THOMAS WILSON*

Type of Vessel	Steel whaleback bulk freighter
Location	Near Duluth Entry, 1 mile offshore
GPS Coordinates	Bow 46°46.957′ N, 92°04.165′ W Stern 46°47.011′ N, 92°04.157′ W
Depth	55 to 70 feet
Dive Rating	Advanced diver

This dive is accessible by boat only. Boaters should post a lookout for large ships that may come into the area. Make sure to post a divers-down flag.

Be cautious when penetrating the wreck. Carry a backup light, in case the primary light source fails. Visibility will vary, being particularly poor after a rain storm. Stay alert to keep from getting entangled in cables, wires, or fishing line. A reconnaissance dive on the outside of the entire ship is required before penetration. When penetrating the wreck, you should maintain proper buoyancy control to avoid stirring up silt. Follow wreck penetration diving procedures as appropriate.

Fig. 57: McDougal patent anchor from the *Thomas Wilson*, next to the Lakewalk in Canal Park. Photo by Stephen B. Daniel.

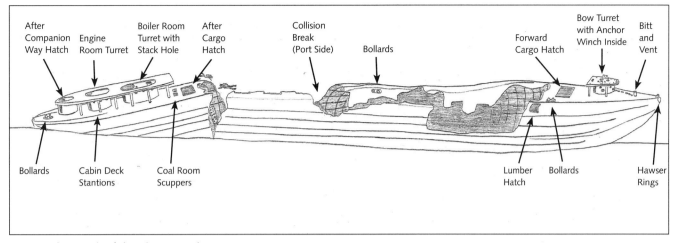

Fig. 58: The wreck of the *Thomas Wilson*. Drawing by Stephen B. Daniel.

Diving Safety near the Duluth Ship Canal

Several shipwrecks are located in or close to the ship canal. Ship and boat traffic may be moving through the canal at various times. Boaters and divers alike should use caution when diving shipwrecks in the vicinity of the ship canal. Dive boats should always have a lookout onboard while divers are underwater; the lookout can take appropriate action as necessary when large ships are in the area. The pilot should be prepared to warn an approaching ship by marine radio or move the boat if the situation warrants it. The divers-down flag should be displayed on the boat. When diving you should take along a signal device to help the boat find you if it has to move before you surface.

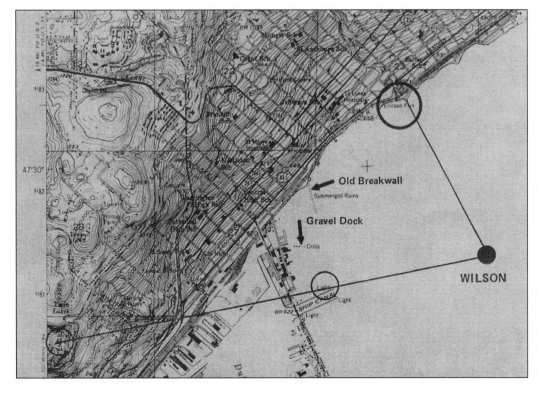

Map 7: *Thomas Wilson* shipwreck site alignment. Look toward Duluth, and sight along the north pier lighthouse, lining it up with Enger Tower up on the hill. Look to the right, across toward the Duluth shoreline, and locate Leif Erikson Park. Check the coordinates, and the wreck should appear on the depth finder. Courtesy of Lake Superior Maritime Collection, University of Wisconsin–Superior.

Fig. 59: The *Wilson*'s porthole opening allows view of interior of forward turret. Photo by Tamara Thomsen.

Fig. 60: Fairlead near bollards was used to guide lines that secured ship at dock in port. Photo by Tamara Thomsen.

Fig. 61: Bollards were used to secure dock lines when in port. Photo by Tamara Thomsen.

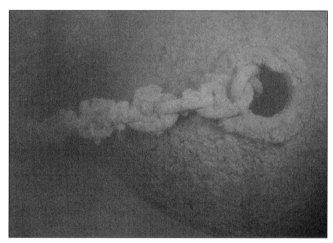

Fig. 62: Anchor chain extends from inside the forward turret to the side of the hull. Photo by Tamara Thomsen.

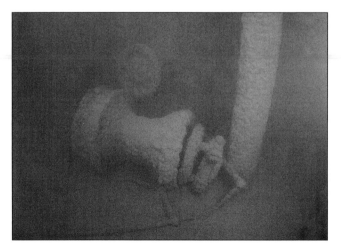

Fig. 63: Capstan (lying on its side) may have been used as a backup for the winch inside the turret. Photo by Tamara Thomsen.

Fig. 64: Fairlead on top of turret used to guide dock lines to bollards nearby. Photo by Tamara Thomsen.

Fig. 65: Posts hold turret deck in place. Photo by Tamara Thomsen.

Fig. 66: Capstan is overturned on forward turret deck. Photo by Tamara Thomsen.

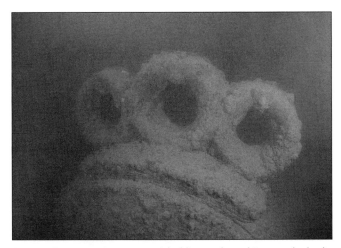

Fig. 67: Bow mooring eyes guided lines when ship was docked in port. Photo by Tamara Thomsen.

A. C. Adams, Lester River

The *A. C. Adams* was a wooden tugboat with a single screw (propeller) built in 1881. M. M. Drake, a master builder, constructed the small vessel at Union Drydock Company in Buffalo, New York.[27] The tug was sixty-two feet long with a beam of sixteen feet and a hold depth of nine feet. The tug grossed a little over forty-one tons. It was powered by a single-cylinder, high-pressure, non-condensing steam engine. The tug was constructed with a single deck but no masts. Its superstructure included a pilothouse and cabin extending aft over the machinery.

The *Adams* worked as a tug around the Buffalo area for about a year. It was sold to J. H. Gillett of Marquette, Michigan, in 1882. It operated in the Marquette area until 1890, when it was sold to Edward Smith and John Fee of Duluth, Minnesota. They formed the Smith and Fee Company of Duluth in 1891. In 1893, they sold the *Adams* to B. B. Inman of Duluth. The Inman Tug Company operated the steam tug until 1899. The Union Towing and Wrecking Company, a division of Great Lakes Towing Company, purchased the *Adams* in 1899. This company was the last owner of the tug until it was scuttled in the early 1920s.

Several rescue episodes involved the *Adams* during its years of service on the Great Lakes. It helped rescue ten crewmen from the 190-foot schooner *Alva Bradley* of Cleveland when it was driven onto the shoals off Shot Point during a storm on October 23, 1887. The *Adams* also tried to rescue the crew of the 137-foot schooner *Reed Case* on October 19, 1888, near Portage Station. It was unsuccessful, however, and lifesavers had to use their surfboat to rescue the sailors from the ship, which had run up on shore. The *Adams* was able to pull the stranded schooner off the shore the next day, but the

Fig. 68: Tug *A. C. Adams* entering Duluth Ship Canal around late 1890s. Courtesy of Minnesota Historical Society/State Historic Preservation Office.

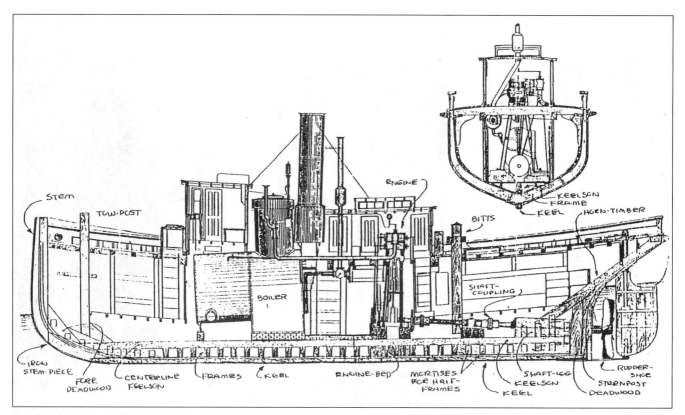

Fig. 69: The *Julian V. O'Brian*, a steam tug similar to the *Adams*. Courtesy of Historical Collections of the Great Lakes, Bowling Green State University, Ohio.

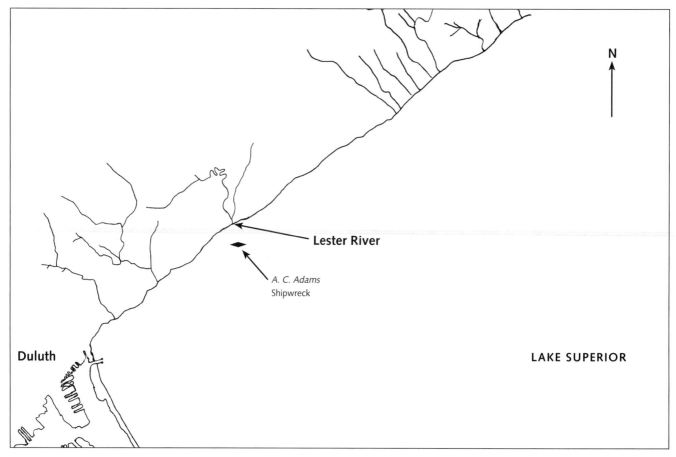

Map 8: The *A. C. Adams* wreck lies off the mouth of the Lester River, about a mile from shore. Drawn by Stephen B. Daniel.

ship capsized and broke up as the tow neared the Portage Ship Canal.

The tug ran aground in fog while towing the schooner *Monteray* near Whitefish Point on June 19, 1889. The incident resulted in only a broken propeller for the *Adams*, but the schooner was heavily damaged and later abandoned. The *Adams* was involved in a collision at Superior, Wisconsin, on June 26, 1892.[28] The tug was used as a floating workshop from the early 1900s until the end of its useful life.

THE SCUTTLING

The propeller and some engine parts were removed from the *Adams* before it was scuttled in the lake between 1921 and 1923.

The wreck was discovered in 1990 off the mouth of the Lester River during a survey by the U.S. Army Corps of Engineers. Ken Merryman, a diver and one of the founders of the GLSPS, was assisting with the survey and found the tug in 118 feet of water.

THE SHIPWRECK

The *Adams* sits in a shallow hole on the lake bottom. Wood planking covers most of the sides of the hull,

except the port quarter. Most of the wood deck boards are also still in place, except behind the engine, where the wooden deck beams (spaced twelve inches) and frames of the tug are visible. The cylindrical fire tube boiler can be seen in front of the steam engine. A bulkhead and some small pieces of the superstructure are off the starboard side of the tug. Other debris, consisting of some planking attached to two-by-four frames, is also scattered nearby. The *Adams* was nominated to the National Register of Historic places in 1992.

DIVING THE *A. C. ADAMS*

Type of Vessel	Wooden tugboat
Location	Near Lester River (east of Duluth), 1 mile offshore
GPS Coordinates	46°49.182' N, 91°59.301' W
Depth	115 feet
Dive Rating	Advanced diver

This dive is accessible by boat only. Use care when setting your anchor to avoid possible damage to the wooden wreck. Post a lookout for large ships that may come into the area, and make certain a divers-down flag is posted.

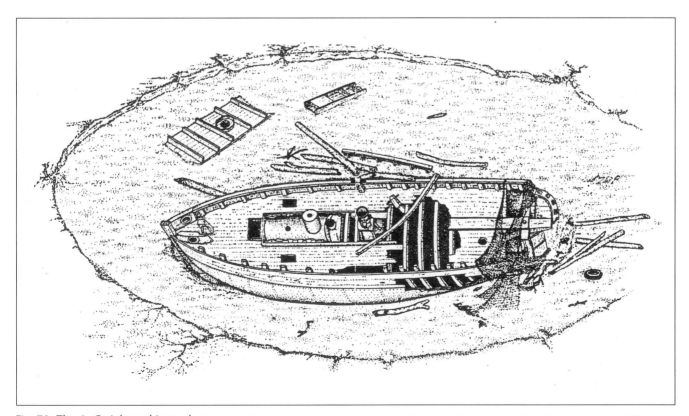

Fig. 70: **The *A. C. Adams* shipwreck.** Drawing by Tidewater Atlantic Research, courtesy of Minnesota Historical Society/State Historic Preservation Office.

Fig. 71: Port-side hull section includes rub rails. Photo by Tamara Thomsen.

Fig. 72: Steam engine is intact on *A.C. Adams*. Photo by Tamara Thomsen.

Fig. 73: Ken Merryman pauses before diving the *A. C. Adams* from his boat, the *Heyboy*. Photo by Stephen B. Daniel.

The wreck site has very limited visibility (sometimes less than five feet), since this site is off the mouth of a river. A backup light is recommended. Use proper buoyancy, and be careful not to stir up silt around the wreck. Since the tugboat is rather small, you should not try to penetrate the hull. Use caution near the port quarter, where fish netting is draped from the fantail of the tug over the side of the hull. The old wooden structure of the tug is very fragile, so look, but don't touch!

Mayflower, Lester River

The *Mayflower* was a 230-ton wooden scow-schooner 147 feet in length. The broad, squared-off shape of the bow enabled it to carry more cargo than a ship of the same size with a sharply pointed bow. The *Mayflower* sailed around the west end of Lake Superior in the late 1800s. On June 2, 1891, it was carrying a cargo of sandstone

from Portage Entry. Some of the sandstone blocks were stacked on the deck.

THE SINKING

The sails were full as the *Mayflower* prepared to approach the Superior Harbor. Captain Zirbest ordered the crew to lower the sails.[29] The ship broached to the moderate seas that were driven by a northeasterly wind. The cargo shifted, causing the ship to capsize. Three sailors from the *Mayflower* were saved by the tug *Cora A. Sheldon* when it hurried to the scene, but Captain Zirbest drowned after he was unable to hold on to the line that had been tossed to him. The *Mayflower* was a total loss, valued at $9,000.

The ship remained undisturbed on the bottom until it was discovered in the 1990s by Duluth diver Jerry

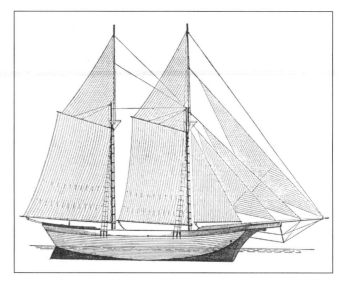

Fig. 74: Drawing of a scow-schooner similar to the *Mayflower*. Courtesy of Lake Superior Maritime Collection, University of Wisconsin–Superior.

Fig. 75: The *Chaska*, a scow-schooner built in Duluth in 1869, similar to the *Mayflower*. Courtesy of Lake Superior Maritime Collection, University of Wisconsin–Superior.

Buchanan. Because of its depth and the poor visibility of the location, few divers visit the *Mayflower*.

THE SHIPWRECK

The wreck sits upright at a ninety-foot depth. Visibility can be very poor because of its proximity to Lester River.

The anchors of the *Mayflower* are still in place on each side of the bow, and the winch also remains in the bow. Be careful when dropping anchor, since you can easily hook the chains of the *Mayflower's* anchors, which are difficult to unhook from in a strong wind.

Many of the sandstone blocks are piled on top of each other. The gunnel rails of the ship's hull are visible on each side. They splay away from the center of the ship, perhaps as a result of the ship hitting the bottom with a heavy load. The past 113 years have filled the vessel with a lot of sand and silt. The square bow and stern fantail are intact and upright, while the midship section of the hull is not.

The tiller and some pulleys from the boom sheet may be seen at the stern. A large square hole in the deck may once have been covered by the cabin structure. Wooden bollards are located on the side at the starboard quarter.

DIVING THE *MAYFLOWER*

Type of Vessel	Wooden scow-schooner
Location	Near Lester River (east of Duluth), 2 miles offshore
GPS Coordinates	46°48.195' N, 92°00.663' W
Depth	90 feet
Dive Rating	Advanced diver

This dive is accessible by boat only. Rice Point Landing, under the Blatnik Bridge, is the closest launch site. Use care when setting your anchor to avoid possible damage to the wooden wreck. Post a lookout for large ships that

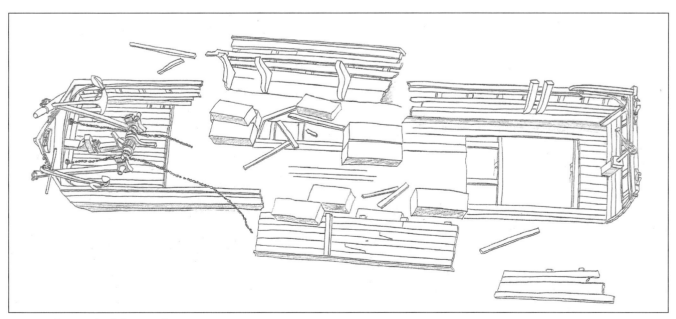

Fig. 76: The wreck of the *Mayflower*. Drawing by Stephen B. Daniel.

may come into the area, and make certain to use a divers-down flag.

The shipwreck site has very limited visibility (sometimes less than a foot), since this site is off the mouth of a river. A backup light is recommended. Use proper buoyancy, and be careful not to stir up silt around the wreck. Penetration is not possible, as there is not much hull structure remaining.

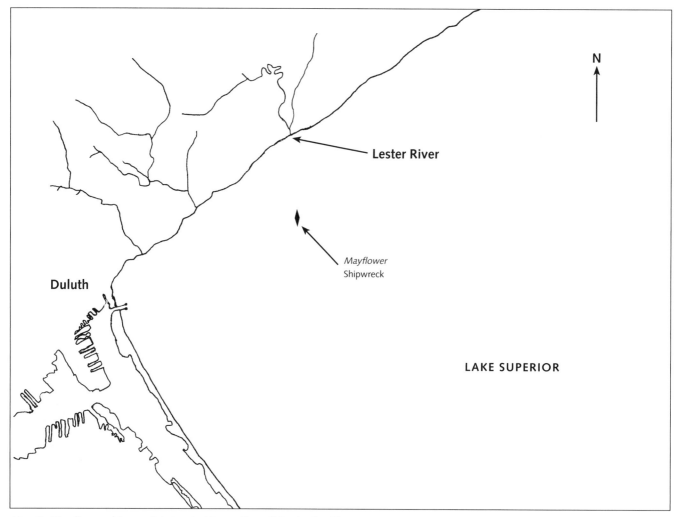

Map 9: *Mayflower* shipwreck is located two miles off the Lester River. Drawn by Stephen B. Daniel.

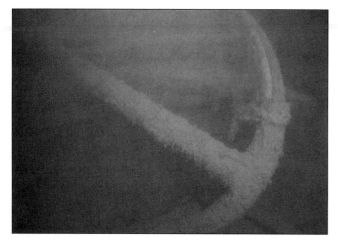

Fig. 77: Huge anchors are secured to each side of the bow.
Photo by Tamara Thomsen.

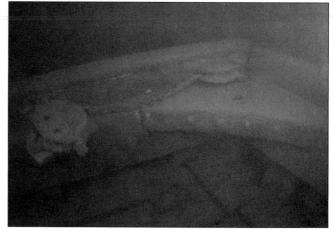

Fig. 78: Blocks (pulleys) in stern quarters once held sheets that controlled boom movement. Photo by Tamara Thomsen.

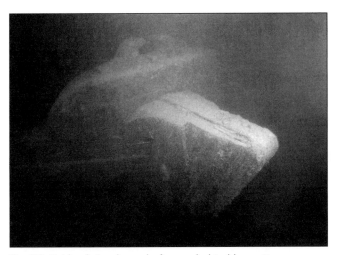

Fig. 79: Fairlead stands ready for use behind bow stem.
Photo by Tamara Thomsen.

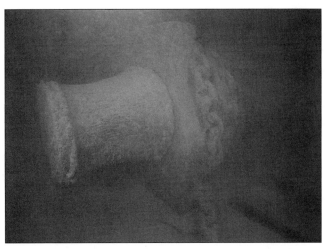

Fig. 80: Warping head on side of winch was used to haul in heavy dock lines. Anchor chain is wound around winch.
Photo by Tamara Thomsen.

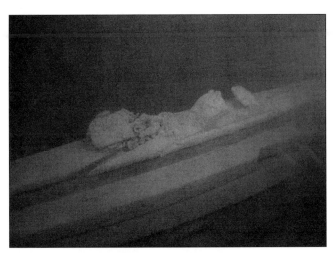

Fig. 81: Block is attached to starboard fairlead at stern of ship.
Photo by Tamara Thomsen.

Fig. 82: Part of the rail near the stern. Photo by Tamara Thomsen.

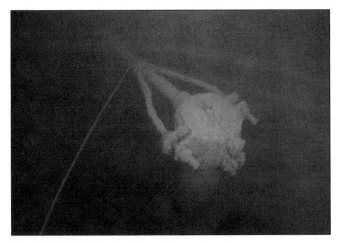

Fig. 83: Tiller is attached to rudder post at stern. Photo by Tamara Thomsen.

Underwater Geology

Lava Terraces, Brighton Beach, Duluth

Brighton Beach is located in Kitchi Gammi Park, on the northeast end of Duluth (just after crossing the Lester River). The site can be reached by turning off Congdon Boulevard (Highway 61) onto Brighton Beach Road. Parking is available along the side of the road.

DIVING THE LAVA TERRACES

Type of Interest	Unusual lava formations
Location	Brighton Beach, northeastern Duluth
Depth	25 feet
Depth	Novice diver

You may find agates embedded in the lava terraces in twenty-five feet of water or less.[30] Do not remove the stones because you may damage the terraces. You can buy polished agates at many local stores along the North Shore.

Lava Flow Formations, Stony Point

The shoreline of the lake in this area was formed more than a billion years ago by basalt lava erupting through the Mid-Continental Rift.[31] Erosion by storms and winter ice buildup over the years has resulted in interesting rock formations, which extend a short distance into the lake. (See map 11, p. 42.)

DIVING THE LAVA FORMATIONS

Type of Interest	Unusual lava formations, possible wreckage from tugboat
Location	Off Scenic Highway 61 and Stony Point Road
Depth	30–40 feet
Dive Rating	Novice diver

This is a shallow dive that is accessible from shore or by boat. A gravel road extends off of Old North Shore Road toward the lake and follows the point. Follow the

Fig. 84: The large fissure in the lava formation at Stony Point. Photo by Stephen B. Daniel.

Fig. 85: Beach provides easy entry to the water. Photo by Stephen B. Daniel.

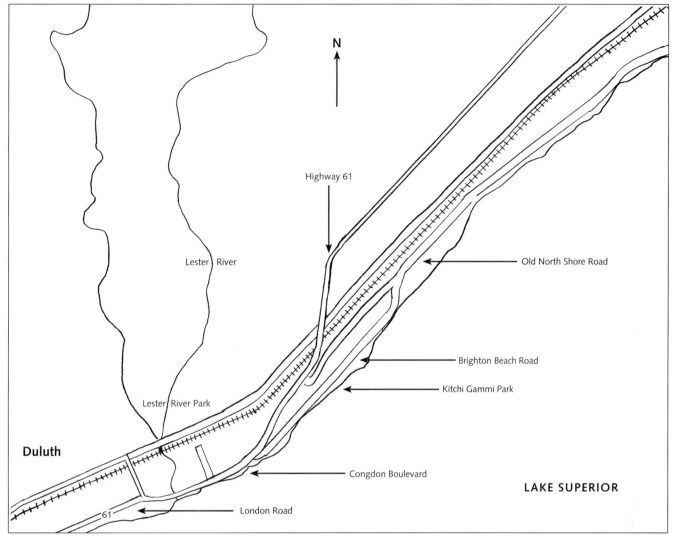

Map 10: Lava terraces are located near Brighton Beach. Drawn by Stephen B. Daniel.

road until the stony beach is visible, and park off to the side. The crevasse dive site can be accessed by swimming along the shore. Be sure to use a divers-down flag.

The best diving is on the northeast side of the point. An alert diver might happen across some agates imbedded in these lava flows as well. Remember not to try to remove them, since you can damage the formations.

While looking at the lava flows, keep an eye out for wreckage from the *Osprey*, a sixty-two-foot, fifty-six-ton small fish tug owned by John Wanless of Duluth.[32] The *Osprey* caught fire on April 13, 1915, and was run up on the shore by its captain. All three of the crew were thus able to escape safely. It burned to the waterline and may have been pulled away from the shore, where it sank nearby. The fire resulted in a complete loss of the fish tug, which was valued at $10,000.[33] The wreckage of the tug has not yet been found.

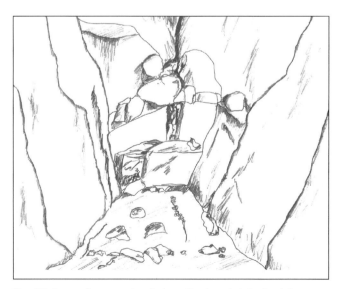

Fig. 86: Large fissure extends from the beach into the lake. Drawing by Stephen B. Daniel.

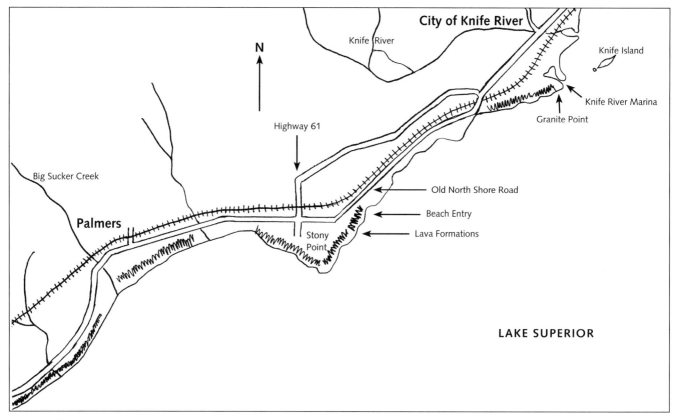

Map 11: **Stony Point is accessible from shore.** Drawn by Stephen B. Daniel.

Shipwrecks in Lake Superior near Knife Island

Onoko

The *Onoko* was an iron 287-foot bulk freight steamer with a beam of 38.8 feet. It was built at Radcliff's yard in Cleveland, Ohio, and launched in February 1882.[34] It grossed 2,164 tons and was one of the largest ships of its type at that time, with two decks and four masts with sails. Its double bottom could carry water ballast, and it also had two watertight bulkheads. The *Onoko* was constructed for Captain Phillip Minch of the Minch Transportation Company, part of the Kingsman Steamship Company, and a group of investors from Cleveland. The *Onoko*'s steam engine consisted of two fore and aft compound cylinders capable of producing nine hundred horsepower at seventy-five revolutions per minute. Steam power was provided to the *Onoko* by two tubular boilers that were eight feet eight inches by eighteen feet in size.

As the first iron-hulled bulk freighter ever built, the *Onoko* was the largest ship on the Great Lakes for ten years and the forerunner of the steel freighters in use today.[35] It broke many records for bulk cargoes during the years of its operation.

While the *Onoko* had a successful shipping career, it was involved in a few accidents. On the foggy night of May 16, 1896, it rammed and sank the schooner *Mary D. Ayer* in Lake Michigan near Racine, Wisconsin. Damage to the *Onoko* was slight, but five of the crew of the *Ayer* went down with their ship. In 1910, on a snowy December 1, the *Onoko* ran aground on Southeast Shoal in Lake Erie, sixty miles below Amherstburg, Ontario. Tugs were able to pull it off the shoal without much damage to the hull. Then, in a prelude to the outcome of its last voyage,

Fig. 88: The *Onoko* with its four masts around 1895 at the Great Northern Elevator in Superior, Wisconsin. Courtesy of Douglas County Historical Society, Superior, Wisconsin.

Fig. 87: *Onoko* under steam and sail in 1920 painting. Courtesy of Kenneth E. Thro Collection, Lake Superior Maritime Collection, University of Wisconsin–Superior.

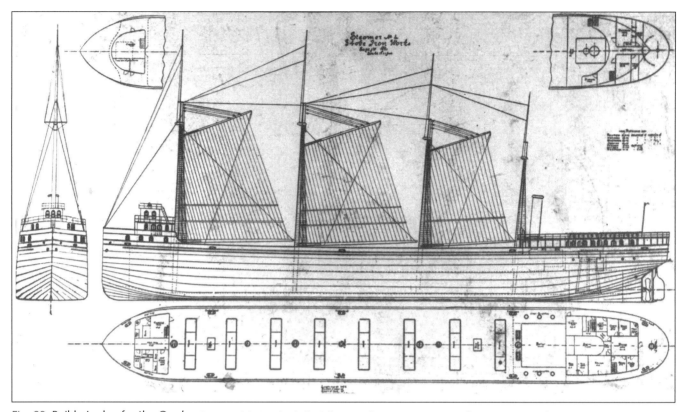

Fig. 89: Builder's plan for the *Onoko*. Courtesy of C. Patrick Labadie Collection, Lake Superior Maritime Collection, University of Wisconsin–Superior.

Fig. 90: The *Onoko* in the Soo Locks around 1900. Courtesy of the Great Lakes Historical Society, Vermillion, Ohio.

Fig. 91: Photo taken by an unknown sailor on the Standard Oil Tanker *Reknown*, showing the *Onoko* sinking on September 15, 1915. Courtesy of Historical Collections of the Great Lakes, Bowling Green State University, Ohio.

the *Onoko* ran aground in early September 1915 while departing a grain elevator in Duluth. The big ship was able to free itself and subsequently cleared the harbor.

The Sinking

The *Onoko* left Duluth on September 15, 1915, loaded with a cargo of a hundred thousand bushels of wheat. Captain William Dunn of Cleveland was in command. The large ship was transporting the wheat to Capitol Elevator Company in Toledo, Ohio. Waters on the lake were smooth. After an uneventful hour steaming away from Duluth, Chief Engineer Higgens noticed that water was gushing into the engine room. After starting the bilge pumps, he found himself in waist-deep water and struggled to the ladder, climbing to the deck with difficulty.[36]

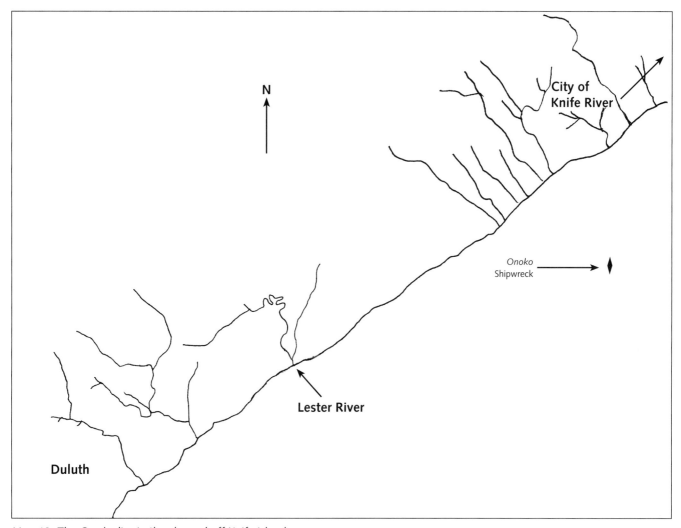

Map 12: The *Onoko* lies in the channel off Knife Island. Drawn by Stephen B. Daniel.

The chief engineer alerted the captain, who, after a quick assessment, surmised that a plate may have fallen from the hull, flooding the entire stern of the ship. He ordered the crew to abandon ship. The sixteen crewmen and a passenger gathered their belongings, along with a pet dog, lowered the lifeboats, and rowed to safety. The Standard Oil Company tanker *Reknown* rushed to the scene and took the *Onoko* crew and passenger aboard. They heard an explosion on the *Onoko* and watched as its bow tipped up into the air and the ship turned end-over-end. The old ship stood up in two hundred feet of water, the hatch covers blew off, and it settled upside down on its deck while sinking. The loss amounted to $160,000—$50,000 for the ship and $110,000 for the wheat cargo.

FINDING THE SHIPWRECK

Divers Jerry Eliason of Scanlon, Minnesota, and Kraig Smith of Rice Lake, Wisconsin, conducted extensive re-search on the *Onoko* and then spent considerable time searching the lake southeast of Knife River, Minnesota, with a depth finder. They found the wreck on April 10, 1988. The large ship lies upside down on the bottom, with its stern pushed into the mud. The hull is broken nearly in half near the stern, in front of the boilers.

DIVING THE ONOKO

Type of Vessel	Iron bulk freighter
Location	South of Knife Island, in the shipping channel
Depth	220 feet
Dive Rating	Technical diver

This dive is accessible by boat only. The closest launch site is the boat ramp at Knife River Marina. Make sure your boat is secure when you anchor near the wreck.

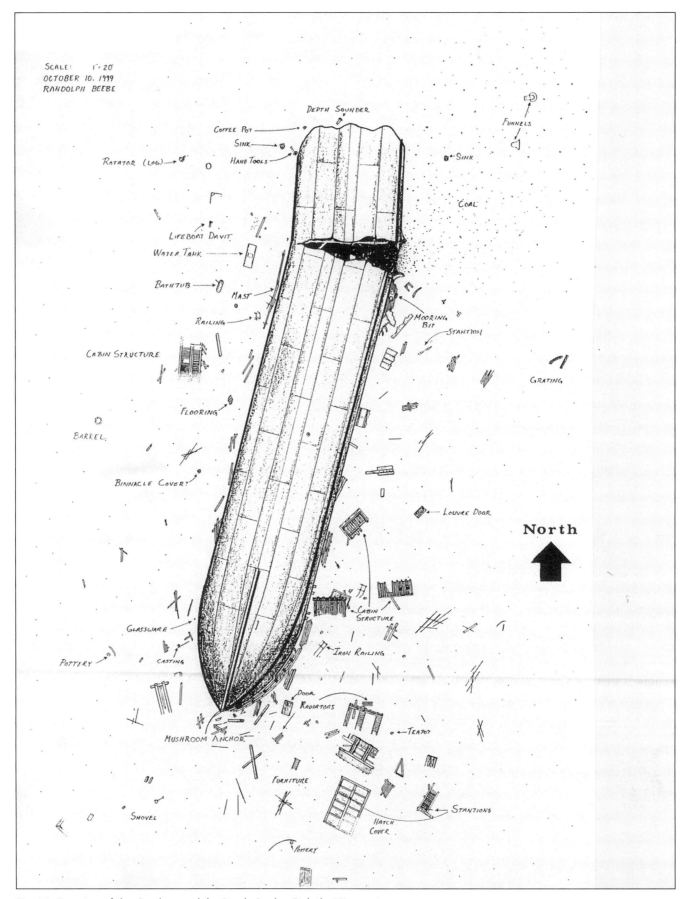

Fig. 92: Drawing of the *Onoko* wreck by Randy Beebe, Duluth, Minnesota.

 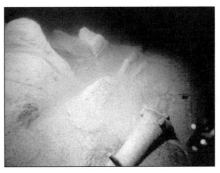 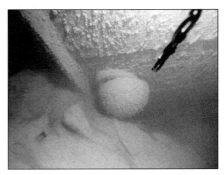

Figs. 93–95 (left to right): A bathtub in debris field by stern of the *Onoko*, a brass pedestal that may be from a sounding machine lying near the wreck, an inverted bow with mushroom anchor. Since this shipwreck is so deep, few may ever have an opportunity to visit it. These photos were taken using a drop camera with lights suspended on a cable from a boat. Courtesy of Jerry Eliason, Scanlon, Minnesota.

Post a lookout for large ships that may come into the area, and make certain a divers-down flag is posted.

This wreck dive is extremely difficult because of the depth, the low water temperature, the current, and poor visibility (sometimes less than one foot). Only properly trained and equipped technical divers should consider diving this shipwreck.

Many artifacts are located in the debris field around the shipwreck. These belong to the State of Minnesota, and it is illegal to remove them. Look at, but do not take, artifacts that you may find near the wreck. The *Onoko* shipwreck has been protected since it was listed on the National Register of Historic Places on August 29, 1992.

Thomas Friant

The *Thomas Friant* was originally built to carry passengers and package freight. The 96-foot-long wooden steamer was launched at Grand Haven, Michigan, in 1884 with a gross tonnage of 83 tons.[37] The *Friant* provided passenger excursion service on Lake Michigan in the late 1880s between the Michigan cities of Harbor Springs, Petoskey, Charlevoix, and East Jordan. The upper deck was rebuilt in 1891. The ship was moved to Milwaukee in 1897 to haul freight to Port Washington. It ferried passengers and freight between Waukegan and Chicago from 1898 to 1899, when James McRae and William H. Rowe of Dollar Bay bought it and moved it to Marquette, Michigan.[38] The *Friant* was then rebuilt in 1901 to enclose its lower deck.

The ship encountered some grounding mishaps during its life on the Great Lakes. After changing owners in 1903 and again in 1907, the *Friant* burned at the dock in Sault Ste. Marie in 1908. While listed as lost in 1909, it was rebuilt in 1910. The length was the same, with a beam at 18.6 feet and a depth of hold at 6.5 feet. The tonnage was changed to 70 gross tons.

The ship changed hands three more times, with the last purchasers, Einar Miller and Halvor A. Reiten, both of Bayfield, Wisconsin, buying it in 1923. Miller was listed as the master. They changed the service of the vessel to freight and moved the ship to Duluth, its last home port. With a crew of four the *Friant* transported freight on the

Fig. 96: The *Thomas Friant* pushes through ice on Lake Superior. Courtesy of Lake Superior Maritime Collection, University of Wisconsin–Superior.

western end of Lake Superior and later switched to the commercial fishing trade.

THE SINKING

The owners decided to use the *Friant* to generate additional revenue during the winter of 1924. On January 6, they departed Port Wing, Wisconsin, with a small group of commercial fishermen from Cornucopia, Wisconsin. The fishermen wanted to try deep-water net fishing along the south shore of the western end of Lake Superior.[39] The day was bitterly cold, with ice forming on the open lake near the south shoreline. While sailing about nine miles out from Port Wing, the *Friant* encountered thickening ice, which cut the hull and started a leak. The crew worked the bilge pumps as the captain tried to move the boat toward the Minnesota North Shore, as the south shore of the lake had become impassable.

The leak grew in intensity as the ship moved into deeper water. The captain headed toward Knife River, but the pumps could not keep up with the incoming water. As the ship started to sink, the fishermen, captain, and crew abandoned ship and rowed to the Minnesota shore in the single lifeboat. The *Friant* slipped below the surface as they pulled away. After several hours of hard rowing in water surrounded by ice flows, all arrived safely ashore near Knife River.

FINDING THE *THOMAS FRIANT*

The *Friant* wreck remained undisturbed for eighty years. In the summer of 2004, several shipwreck hunters were searching for the *Robert Wallace* in Lake Superior about twelve miles east-southeast of Knife River. Jerry Eliason, Randy Beebe, Ken Merryman (all from Minnesota) and Kraig Smith (from Wisconsin) had spent over ten years searching for the *Wallace*. In late July 2004, they thought they had found it. The group expanded to include technical divers Bob Nelson and Ron Benson.

On August 1, 2004, the group anchored over the wreck site and extended drop cameras below the boat. Images from drop cameras on previous trips had led the shipwreck hunters to believe they had found the *Wallace*. This time however, the video transmitted images of a ship with features that did not look like they belonged

Figs. 97–100 (top to bottom): A diver examines the compass binnacle on the forward deck. The ship's wheel inside the pilothouse. A diver explores the *Friant*'s engine room, where the engine is still in place. The *Friant*'s bell is mounted in front of the pilothouse. All courtesy of Ken Merryman, Fridley, Minnesota.

Exploring a Newly Discovered Shipwreck

The topside crew of a shipwreck hunt is very busy when a hit is found on the side-scan sonar. The crew makes several passes to mark the location of the shipwreck. Marker buoys are dropped over the side of the search boat, and equipment is prepared for the dive. The boat crew sets the anchor, which is carefully positioned so that it doesn't damage the wreck. The divers prepare their equipment for the dive, with tenders remaining above to handle the divers' potential needs. While the divers are below on the shipwreck, the surface crew monitors their position by observing their bubbles and watching the time that they are underwater. The surface crews are also trained divers. The event is documented by video both above and below the surface.

Figs. 101–103 (left, right, and below): Jay Cole readies the underwater video camera. A video crew records a dive topside. Divers return to the surface after an exploratory dive. All courtesy of Ron Johnson, Golden Valley, Minnesota.

to a large bulk freighter. Using rebreathers, divers followed the anchor line to a depth of over three hundred feet. They found the vessel below to be smaller than a freighter, resembling a commercial fishing tug. They secured the anchor and carefully proceeded to explore the intact wreck. The artifacts that remained onboard proved that this was a virgin shipwreck. The dive team rose to the pilothouse toward the bow of the ship. Their lights illuminated the name board, on which was painted "Thomas Friant" in white letters. Several stamped metal fishing licenses were observed over the doorway to the pilothouse, dating the ship to the 1920s. The team found a compass binnacle in an unusual location on the forward deck. The ship's bell was found in place as well.

The dive team found many interesting and well-preserved artifacts on board the *Friant*. The ship is upright and virtually intact, with everything in place from the day it sank. The divers were careful not to disturb any of the artifacts or the structure of the ship. They believe that historic shipwrecks are best preserved by leaving everything as they found it so that other visiting divers and historians may have an opportunity to experience the same enjoyment of viewing maritime history where it occurred. The group will work with the state authorities to protect the shipwreck and its well-preserved historic artifacts in an appropriate manner. Until then, the location will not be publicized.

Benjamin Noble

The *Benjamin Noble* was built by the Detroit Shipbuilding Company in Wyandotte, Michigan. It was a 239-foot, 1,481-gross-ton steel bulk freighter with a beam of slightly over 42 feet and a single screw. It was crane-equipped and launched on April 28, 1909. Its small size helped it navigate the Welland Canal locks in Canada, between the St. Lawrence River and the upper Great Lakes. The *Noble* had one deck and two masts. A triple-expansion steam engine powered the ship, producing 870 horsepower at ninety revolutions per minute. The ship had two Scotch boilers measuring 11.5 by 12 feet to produce steam power. The Detroit Sulphite Fibre Company was the first owner, intending to use the ship to transport pulpwood. The ship's hull was built higher above the deck on each side to accommodate this type of cargo. The ship also frequently carried cargoes of railroad steel and coal.[40]

The *Benjamin Noble* sailed the eastern Great Lakes for several years until it encountered a severe storm with gale-force winds beginning on April 27, 1914. The thirty-one-year-old captain, John Eisenhardt of Milwaukee, who was employed by Capitol Transportation Company, was the master on what was to be the ship's last voyage. It was heavily loaded with a cargo of rails intended for the Great Northern Railroad at Superior. The young captain planned to hug the shoreline all the way to Duluth to assure the safe arrival of his overloaded ship. The *Noble* was last seen near the Keeweenaw Peninsula of Michigan as it headed toward the west end of Lake Superior.

The ship rounded Devils Island, where it encountered a northeast storm that increased in intensity as the ship continued on.[41] Several reports in the papers at that time surmised that the ship was headed to Two Harbors or Duluth; other ships saw it at various times during the storm. But the current location of the ship and its intact but heavily damaged hull support a different theory. The *Noble*'s decks were awash with heavy seas it encountered during the storm, and its extremely heavy cargo caused

Fig. 104: The *Benjamin Noble*. Courtesy of Lake Superior Maritime Collection, University of Wisconsin–Superior.

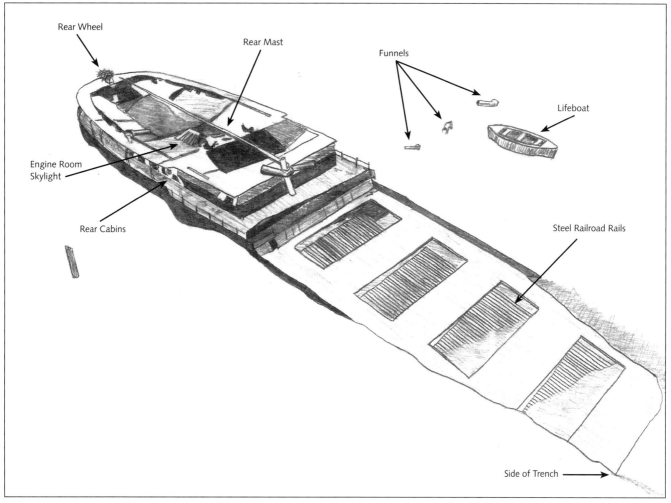

Fig. 105: Steel railroad rails in the cargo holds confirm this is the wreck of the long lost *Benjamin Noble*. Drawing by Stephen B. Daniel, based on underwater photographs by Ken Merryman, Fridley, Minnesota.

it to sail low in the water. The scuppers in the sides of the raised hull were not large enough to let the water drain overboard before the next wave washed over the ship's deck. The captain may also have encountered a huge wave as he tried to change course and seek better weather. The wave would have been too much for the ship's condition, preventing it from recovering and sending it hurtling toward the bottom of the lake.

The *Duluth Herald* reported on April 29, 1914: "That the steamer *Benjamin Noble*, its crew of twenty men and officers and a large cargo of railroad iron were swallowed up in the turbulent waters of Lake Superior last night was made practically certain today when the life saving crew picked up oars, hatches, life belts and other wreckage from the ill-fated steamer off Minnesota Point at about Twenty-first Street."[42]

Several tugs searched the lake between Two Harbors and Duluth for evidence of the *Noble*, but nothing was found. Life-saving crews continued to look along the south shore but could find no other signs of the lost ship. None of the ship's crew were ever recovered; their remains are believed to still be aboard the ship.

FINDING THE *BENJAMIN NOBLE*

Shipwreck hunters discovered the location of the *Benjamin Noble* in October 2004. They had been canvassing the bottom of the western end of Lake Superior over the previous ten years. Jerry Eliason of Scanlon, Minnesota, used side-scan sonar to locate the ship. Ken Merryman of Fridley, Minnesota, Randy Beebe of Duluth, and Kraig Smith of Rice Lake, Wisconsin, used drop cameras to observe details on board the ship in order to confirm its identity.[43] The divers made two more dives in 2005 to video record the site and found extensive damage to the ship, which lies in a trench with its forward end covered in bottom clay. Many rows of railroad rails are visible in its cargo holds.

DIVING THE *BENJAMIN NOBLE*

Type of Vessel	Steel bulk freighter
Location	About 8 miles south-southeast of Knife River
Depth	360 feet
Dive Rating	Technical diver

The shipwreck is located about eight miles east-southeast of Knife River. The vessel is at a depth of over 360 feet, which requires special considerations for diving equipment and diving procedures. The heavy load of steel rails, combined with the seas that submerged the ship's deck and the propeller, which continued to turn, drove the vessel to the bottom with considerable force. The rear cabins are partially collapsed as a result of exploding boilers and the tremendous force of the deep water the ship encountered as it plunged quickly to the bottom. According to Jerry Eliason, the ship sits in a deep furrow it plowed with its own hull as it dove into the lake bottom. The mast is broken and lies across the rear cabin roof. Near the front of the roof is a funnel, with other funnels off the port side of the ship's stern near a lifeboat.

The cargo of railroad rails is visible through each of the open hatches of the cargo holds.

Only divers who have the equipment, training, and experience to dive at this depth should attempt this dive. Please respect the site. Remember that the 1987 Abandoned Shipwreck Law gives the State of Minnesota ownership of all underwater artifacts of vessels not privately owned that are located in the waters off its shores. This shipwreck was nominated to the National Register of Historic Places on May 15, 2007. It was approved in November 2007 and is now listed on the registry. This makes it illegal to remove any artifacts from the site.

Niagara

The *Niagara* was built as a towing steamer in Detroit and launched in 1872. It was 130 feet long and grossed 276 tons. It was operated as a rafting tug by the Perry Wrecking Company of Sault Ste. Marie.[44] The *Niagara* towed bag booms, a type of raft like a floating fence of logs, from Lake Superior to such places as Bay City, Michigan, where the logs would be sawn into lumber.

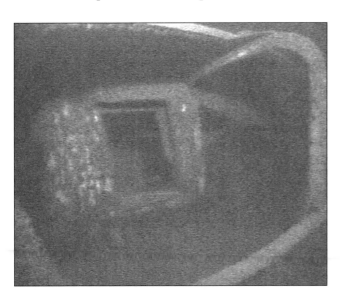

Fig. 106: Drop camera photo of the front of the rear cabins. Courtesy of Jerry Eliason, Scanlon, Minnesota.

Fig. 107: Side-scan sonar image of the *Benjamin Noble* as the ship appears on the bottom today in Lake Superior. Image courtesy of Jerry Eliason, Scanlon, Minnesota.

Fig. 108: View of the port bow of the *Niagara* in the Soo Locks, before 1887. Courtesy of Great Lakes Marine Collection, Milwaukee Public Library / Wisconsin Marine Historical Society.

Fig. 109: The *Niagara* at Bay City, Michigan, around 1887–1889. Courtesy of C. Patrick Labadie Collection, Superior, Wisconsin.

On June 4, 1904, the *Niagara* was on the way to Duluth to pick up a tow of marine construction equipment belonging to Hugo & Tim's before heading to Lake Huron, where a pier was being built. It had trouble navigating because of fog and the heavy influence of magnetic ore in the rock around Knife River. The big tug unknowingly came upon Knife Island and went ashore on the reef. The high swells of the seas began to pound the ship as it listed heavily on the reef. Some women who were in the cabins higher up on the ship were trapped as the vessel started to break up.

The *Niagara*'s whistle shrieked a distress signal, but the trees on the island blocked the view of the stranded ship from residents of the village on shore. Finally, the telegraph operator for the Duluth and Iron Range Railroad saw the masts protruding above the island and, hearing the whistle, signaled its office in Two Harbors.

The *Edna G.*, the railroad's tug, was dispatched from the ore docks to rescue the female passengers and the crew. The crew was able to free the women from their quarters and prepared them to leave the sinking ship. The *Edna G.* brought all thirteen of the passengers and crew to safety.

The grinding surf continued to tear at the *Niagara* through the night. The ship came apart and slid down the reef in pieces on the east side of the island. The *Niagara* was a total loss at $12,000. The engine was salvaged by wreckers, along with some other parts of the ship.

THE SHIPWRECK

The wreck consists of four main sections that are positioned on the bottom near each other at about an 80-foot depth. Visibility can be very poor because of the proximity to the Knife River (to the north of the site). About 60 feet of the forward part of the ship have been found. These represent the stem, port, and starboard bow sections and a small starboard rail section. The midship section lies about 150 feet east of the bow in 100 feet of water. The engine was salvaged near the northeast end of the island, with some debris left in this area. The stern section is still missing. The *Niagara* shipwreck was nominated to the National Register of Historic Places in 1992.

DIVING THE *NIAGARA*

Type of Vessel	Wooden rafting tug
Location	East of Knife Island, about 100 feet offshore of the island
GPS Coordinates	46°56.679' N, 91°46.358' W
Depth	50–100 feet
Dive Rating	Advanced diver

This dive is accessible by boat only. The closest launch site is the public boat ramp at the Knife River Marina. Be aware of the rocks on each end of the island, and take

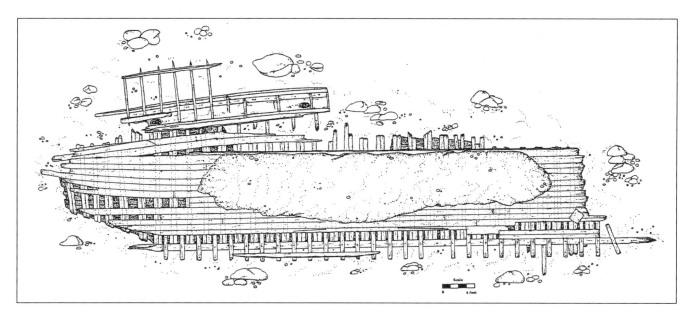

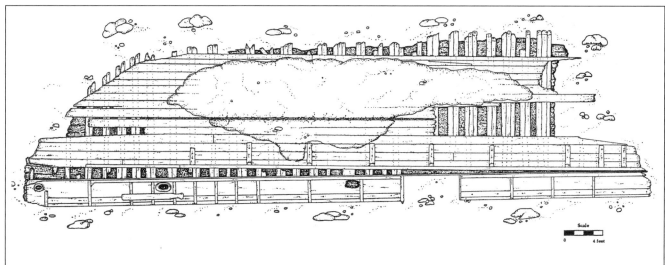

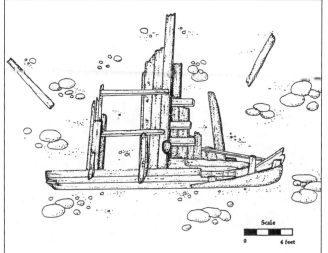

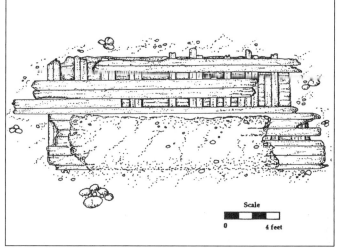

Figs. 110–113: (From top to bottom, left to right) Starboard side section, port side section, stem section, and starboard rail section of the *Niagara* shipwreck on the east side of Knife Island. Drawings by Tidewater Atlantic Research, courtesy of Minnesota Historical Society / State Historic Preservation Office.

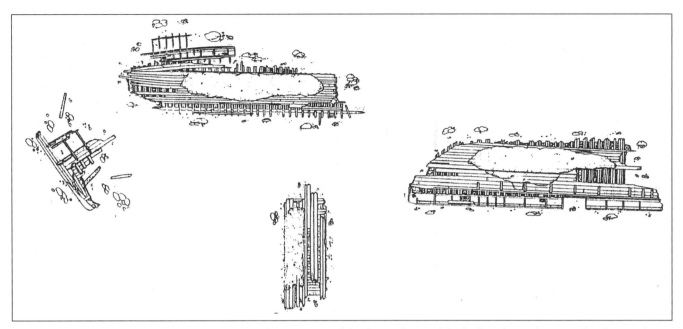

Fig. 114: Plan view of the *Niagara* shipwreck. The four sections of the forward part of the hull are located near each other on the bottom. The stern sections have not been located. Drawings by Tidewater Atlantic Research, courtesy of Minnesota Historical Society / State Historic Preservation Office.

care when anchoring to avoid damaging the wood structure of the wreck. Make sure the boat is secure, post a lookout for other boats that may come into the area, and post a divers-down flag.

This wreck dive is relatively flat. The sections are near each other and can be reached by swimming the short distance between them. Visibility can be limited at times, since the shipwreck is located near the mouth of the Knife River. The bow piece is 60 feet deep, the sides are at 80 feet, and the midship section is 100 feet deep. Some metal debris (pipes and possibly some tools from the engine room) may be found if you swim toward the northeast end of the island. Some planks and other metal pieces from the wreck were left by the salvage operation. Another possible dive is the rock wall on the north side of the east end of the island; the wall extends from the surface to the sandy bottom in 50 feet of water.

Fig. 115: View of Knife Island from shore near the Knife River Marina. The shipwreck is located on the opposite side directly out from the center of the island. Photo by Stephen B. Daniel.

Fig. 116: Public ramp at the Knife River Marina. Knife Island is a short distance from the launch. Photo by Stephen B. Daniel.

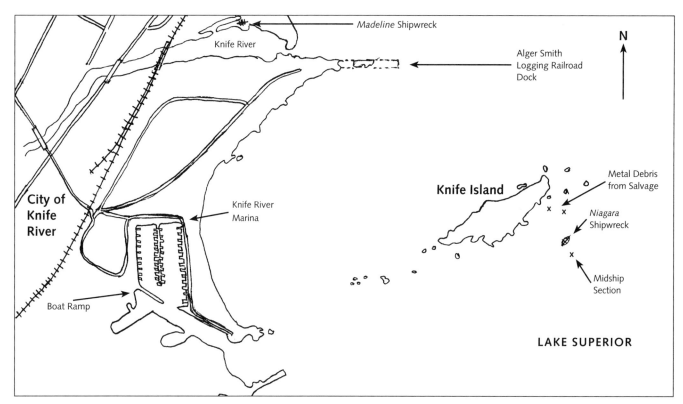

Map 13: The *Niagara* wreck can be found in four sections on the east side of Knife Island. The ruins of the Alger Smith Logging Railroad Dock (see p. 58–60) are located off the mouth of the Knife River, just northwest of Knife Island. Drawn by Stephen B. Daniel.

Fig. 117: A block from the *Niagara* wreckage rests on the fallen hull side. Photo by Tamara Thomsen.

Fig. 118: The severed bow stem is covered with steel plating. Photo by Tamara Thomsen.

Fig. 119: Planking is intact on the port side of the hull. Photo by Tamara Thomsen.

Fig. 120: The hawse hole once guided the anchor chain through the side of the hull. Photo by Tamara Thomsen.

Fig. 121: Iron fitting is secured to the inside of the hull of the *Niagara*. Photo by Tamara Thomsen.

Madeline

The *Madeline* was a forty-foot, twenty-ton merchant schooner launched at Lorraine, Ohio, in 1837.[45] The small schooner was caught in a storm on Lake Superior off the coast of the present-day community of Knife River in 1839. While seeking shelter from the storm, the ship was driven into the mouth of the Knife River by fierce wind and waves and ran aground on the shal-low river bottom, where it remained to rot over the years.

Today a mound of sand and gravel from the river covers its bones on the northeast side of the river mouth. This shipwreck is not a dive site, but it is worth noting as part of the early history of the North Shore.

Fig. 122: The rib structure once supported the upper hull planks. Photo by Tamara Thomsen.

Fig. 124: View of the suspected site of the *Madeline* shipwreck in the mouth of the Knife River. The arrow points to a mounded area covered with river gravel that may have covered the wreck after it deteriorated. Photo by Stephen B. Daniel.

Fig. 123: Frames once held the side of the hull to the bottom of the ship. Photo by Tamara Thomsen.

Point of Interest in Lake Superior at Knife River

Alger Smith Logging Railroad Dock

Just a short distance off the mouth of the Knife River are the ruins of an old concrete dock that once served as a loading dock for lumber hooker ships that would tie up alongside (see map 13, p. 56). The Alger Smith Logging Railroad operated a rail yard until 1920 in the area that is now the Knife River Marina.[46] An old railroad station can still be seen in the nearby village of Knife River. The rail lines once extended over a trestle onto the dock. Pulpwood was cut in the north woods and brought to Knife River. Trains would push loads of logs onto the dock, where they would be loaded onto lumber hooker ships destined for mills in ports around the Great Lakes.[47]

Fig. 125: **Loading coal.** Courtesy of Frank King Collection and U.S. Army Corps of Engineers, Duluth, Minnesota.

Fig. 126: The Duluth and Northern Minnesota No. 14 hauls carloads of white pine logs into Knife River. Courtesy of Frank King Collection.

Fig. 127: Train pushes logs toward the *Lackawanna* at the Knife River dock in 1915. Photo by Roloff, courtesy of the Kenneth E. Thro Collection, University of Wisconsin–Superior.

The dock may also have been used by passengers who boarded the *America*, a packet steamship that carried people and freight along the North Shore before roads for automobiles were built but probably after the logging railroad yard ceased operations. Evidence of this can be observed on the street sign near the railroad tracks by the Knife River Marina. The dock eventually fell into disrepair; the trestle and road leading to it likely washed out gradually during lake storms over the years.

Diving the Alger Smith Logging Railroad Dock

Type of Structure	Concrete with cribs off lake end
Location	Southeast side of mouth of Knife River, about 30 feet offshore
Depth	5–25 feet
Dive	Intermediate diver

This dive is accessible primarily by boat. The closest launch site is the public boat ramp at the Knife River Marina. If you wish to try to dive from shore, remember that the shoreline is private property, so you will need to request permission from the owners. Post a lookout for

other boats that may come into the area, and make certain to post a divers-down flag.

The dock can be easily navigated near the edges, especially on the end near deeper water. Visibility may be limited at times, since the dock is located at the mouth of the Knife River. The best visibility will be in mid to late summer, when the river is running slowly and the currents are less. Look for the cribs off the lake end of the dock. Since the river bottom is sandy, there may not be much else to see; however, lake storms may uncover artifacts from the railroad operations.

Fig. 128: The ruins of the old dock as seen from the rocky shoreline. Photo by Stephen B. Daniel.

Fig. 129: The dock may be reached by swimming from shore after walking along the beach from the marina. Photo by Stephen B. Daniel.

Shipwreck in Lake Superior near Knife River

Robert Wallace

The *Robert Wallace* was a wooden bulk freight steamer launched in Cleveland in 1882. It was 209 feet long and grossed 1,189 tons.[48] The ship experienced a grounding on the beach near Marquette Harbor during a November storm in 1886. It was towing a schooner barge consort, the *David Wallace*, when it was blown off course during blinding snow. Both ships were stranded as a result. The fierce seas limited rescue efforts by local people to shoot a breeches buoy to the ships. This failed, and the U.S. Lifesaving Service from Portage Station, over 110 miles away, was called in.[49]

While the crews huddled in the cabins (both ships were fortunately facing into the gale), the lifesaving service hurried toward them with equipment aboard trains, hampered by heavily drifting snow. When the rescuers got to Marquette, they tried several times to reach the ships with their boat, but had to turn back when the rudder was damaged in the storm. They repaired the rudder and were able to complete the rescue early the next morning. The forward upper cabins of the *Wallace* burned off when a coal stove tipped over. Both cargoes

Fig. 131: The bulk freighter *Robert Wallace* (far right) and its consort *David Wallace* grounded off Marquette, Michigan, during an 1886 November gale. Courtesy of John E. Keast Collection, Lake Superior Maritime Collection, University of Wisconsin–Superior.

of grain had to be lightered (transported by barge) in order to move the ships off the beach. The heavy damage to the *Wallace* was repaired, and it sailed again. The schooner barge sustained less damage and was repaired as well.

The Sinking

On November 17, 1902, the *Wallace* was towing the barge *Ashland* as its consort. Both ships had just left Two Harbors loaded with iron ore. They were reportedly thirteen miles southeast of Two Harbors on a clear night when the *Wallace* hit a log, which tore out the stern post. This jammed the rudder and caused the ship to sink.

As the *Wallace* rapidly filled with water, its crew quickly boarded the *Ashland* when it coasted up to the stricken ship. All hands were rescued, but the ship slipped below the surface of the lake just southeast of Two Harbors. The tug *Edna G.* came to the scene after distress flares were lit by the *Ashland* crew. The *Wallace* pilothouse floated off the ship with the

Fig. 130: *Robert Wallace*. Courtesy of C. Patrick Labadie Collection, Superior, Wisconsin.

lanterns still burning. It was found early the next day by the steamer *Argus.*

The *Robert Wallace* was valued at $40,000 and was owned by Corrigan, McKinney and Company of Cleveland. Unfortunately, the ship was underinsured, making the loss more difficult for the owners.

Finding the *Robert Wallace*

An unidentified source discovered the *Robert Wallace* in late 2006 and reported the location to diver Jay Hanson,

Fig. 132: A diver examines the white lettering spelling out "Robert Wallace" on the stern of the ship. Courtesy of Ken Merryman, Fridley, Minnesota.

who was able to verify the ship during a deep dive to the wreckage on the bottom of Lake Superior. Ken Merryman conducted a dive with Hanson in 2006 and one in 2007 to capture the wreckage on video. Merryman and Bob Olson identified the shipwreck as the *Wallace* through a video shot of the name that was still painted in white on the stern of the ship. The wreck site will soon be nominated to the National Register of Historic Places.

Diving the *Robert Wallace*

Type of Vessel	Wooden bulk freight steamer
Location	Southeast of Two Harbors
Depth	240 feet
Dive	Technical diver

The *Wallace* is a cold, dark, very deep dive. Divers visiting the site have encountered a strong current. The ship is intact in an upright position, and many artifacts are visible on the wreck. Look at but don't touch them, so that other divers may enjoy observing them as well. These artifacts belong to the State of Minnesota; it is illegal to remove them.

Shipwrecks in Lake Superior near Two Harbors

Harriet B.

The *Harriet B.* started out as a car ferry when it was built in Toledo, Ohio, in 1895 as the *Shenango #2*.[50] The wooden ship was 283 feet long and grossed 1,938 tons. Later it was made into a barge and was often used to haul lumber. The ship experienced many mishaps during its time on the lakes. It became known around ports as a "hard-luck" ship (even when it was a car ferry) because of these accidents.

THE SINKING

Heavy fog hung over the lake near Two Harbors on May 3, 1922. The 298-foot-long steamer *C. W. Jacob* was towing the barge *Crete*, followed by the barge *Harriet B.*, both loaded with pulpwood. The steamer and its consorts arrived near Two Harbors a little after one A.M. Because of the foggy conditions, the *Jacob*'s master preferred to wait it out to allow a safer entry into the harbor. The seas were calm, so the ships anchored about a mile off shore, three miles southwest of the breakwater light.[51]

The *Quincy A. Shaw*, a large 504-foot steamer owned

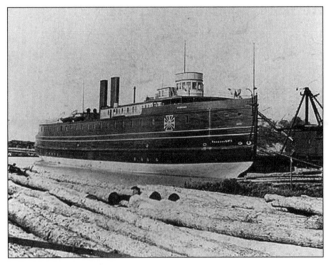

Fig. 134: The *Harriet B.* as a car ferry. Courtesy of Lake Superior Maritime Collection, University of Wisconsin–Superior.

by the M. A. Hanna Company, was moving rapidly on the lake. Emerging from the fog, it slammed into the *Harriet B.* The captain and crew of the *Harriet B.* had less than twenty minutes to abandon ship and board the *Shaw*. The twenty-seven-year-old *Harriet B.* sank in the waters off Two Harbors, with its wheelhouse washing

Fig. 133: The *Harriet B.* Courtesy of Lake Superior Maritime Collection, University of Wisconsin–Superior.

Fig. 135: The *Harriet B.*'s pilothouse with the ship's wheel washed up on the beach at Knife River. Courtesy of Lake Superior Maritime Collection, University of Wisconsin–Superior.

ashore nearby. The *Harriet B.* was valued at more than $25,000 and owned by the Hammermill Paper Company of Erie, Pennsylvania, when it sank. (The *Shaw* was repaired in Ashtabula, Ohio, the next week, as its damage was above the waterline.)

HARRIET B. FOUND

The *Harriet B.* was accidentally discovered early in 2005 during a geological survey of the lake bottom by the crew of the *Blue Heron*, the University of Minnesota-Duluth research ship.[52] The *Blue Heron* crew contacted Randy Beebe and Jerry Eliason, experienced shipwreck hunters who viewed the side-scan sonar images and performed further investigations with drop cameras to confirm the identity of the ship.

DIVING IS NOT RECOMMENDED

The hull of the *Harriet B.* rests in 650 feet of water about three and a half miles east-southeast of Two Harbors. The hull appears to be relatively intact. The depth is too great

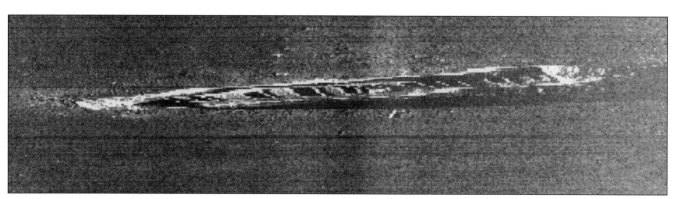

Fig. 136: Side-scan sonar image of the *Harriet B.* shipwreck. Courtesy of Nigel Wattris, captain of the *Blue Heron*.

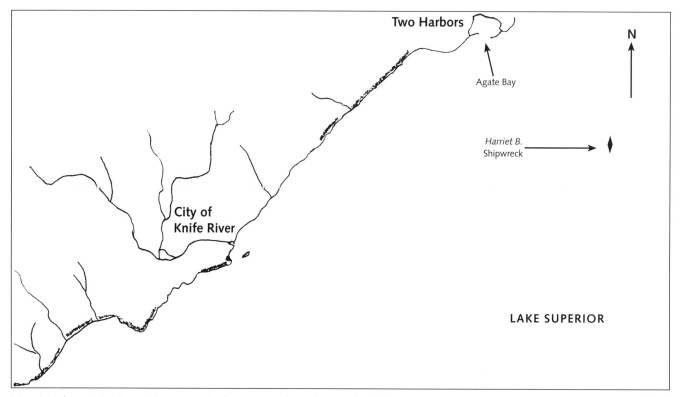

Map 14: The *Harriet B.* rests in extremely deep water about three and a half miles east-southeast of Two Harbors. Drawn by Stephen B. Daniel.

Fig. 137: Underwater image of the mast on the lifeboat from the *Harriet B*. Drop camera photo courtesy of Randy Beebe, Duluth, Minnesota.

for divers to comfortably check out in person. While the technology of the newest diving equipment may accommodate diving at this depth, the decompression time required would be very long. Jerry Eliason commented that a very brief visit (less than ten minutes) to the deep shipwreck would require about eight hours of decompression stops on the way back to the surface to complete the dive safely. The condition of the lake could easily change dramatically during that same period of time, potentially presenting additional challenges to the dive team and support staff. You can most effectively view this shipwreck in underwater drop camera video footage. (A Great Lakes Shipwreck Preservation Society [GLSPS] Dive into the Past shipwreck scuba show will feature a video presentation on this wreck once it is available. The annual show is open to the public and held on the last Saturday of February.)

Samuel P. Ely, West Breakwater

The *Samuel P. Ely* was a three-masted wooden schooner with a single deck built near Detroit at the J. P. Clark Shipyards. The sturdy ship was built of white oak and was launched in 1869. It was 200 feet long, with a beam of 31 feet, and grossed 627 tons. The ship served as a schooner barge on the Great Lakes, hauling cargoes of iron ore and limestone, and was towed behind a steamer as a consort. A towline attached to the large sampson post near its stern could secure another schooner barge as well.

Near the end of October 1896, the *Ely* had finished an upbound trip with a load of limestone, having been towed behind the 250-foot *Hesper*. A second schooner barge, the *Negaunee*, had been in tow behind the *Ely*.

The two schooners unloaded their limestone cargoes in Duluth, while the *Hesper* unloaded coal and picked up a new cargo of wheat.

The *Hesper* then planned to tow the two empty schooner barges to Two Harbors, where they would be loaded with iron ore for a trip to Buffalo, New York. The *Hesper* finished loading grain and left Duluth the morning of October 29, 1896, with the two schooner barges in tow.[53] A tremendous gale began to blow across the lake from the northeast, increasing in intensity as the day wore on. The ships could barely make headway in the driving rain. A trip from Duluth to Two Harbors would normally have taken only two hours, or three at the most. The tow group didn't arrive at Two Harbors until eight P.M.

THE SINKING

The seas were the highest that local residents had ever seen. The *Hesper* had so much difficulty in the dangerous waves that it had to throw off the tow line to the consorts in order to make it safely into the harbor. As soon as the line was let go, the *Ely* was in trouble with the high seas. It dropped anchor but drifted precariously close to the breakwater on the west side of the harbor, dragging its anchors on the way. The tug that came out to help the *Ely* did not arrive soon enough after the towline was cast off. The *Ely* threw another towline to the tug, but it broke immediately. The winds, which were estimated at fifty miles an hour, soon pushed the schooner hard on the breakwater around midnight. A construction scow that had been working in the harbor was on the breakwater when the *Ely* crashed into it. The men on the small scow quickly climbed aboard the larger *Ely* for a better chance

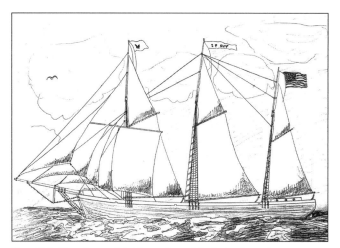

Fig. 138: The *Samuel P. Ely* under sail in Lake Superior. Drawing by Stephen B. Daniel, based on a painting in Two Harbors Lighthouse Museum.

of surviving the gale. The schooner sank alongside the breakwater at three A.M. The men barely had time to climb into the rigging in the darkness to avoid drowning.

Meanwhile, the superintendent of the Duluth and Iron Range Railroad, the company that operated the ore docks where the *Ely* was going to load, telegraphed the U.S. Life Saving Service in Duluth and sent a train to transport them to the *Ely*'s crew. But debris blocked the path of the lifesavers and their equipment as they tried to reach the train tracks. Meanwhile, the train heading toward

Fig. 139: The *Samuel P. Ely* with tugs in the Duluth Ship Canal around 1890. Courtesy of Lake Superior Maritime Collection, University of Wisconsin–Superior.

them encountered tracks that were washed out by the storm and wreckage that blocked its way.[54]

The railroad superintendent, informed of the problem, directed his employees to build bonfires along the front of the harbor. He then sent the captain of the railroad's tug, the *Ella G. Stone*, to acquire a sailboat from a local fisherman to help with the rescue. The *Stone* towed

Fig. 140: The *Ella G. Stone* by the ore docks. Courtesy of Fr. Edward J. Dowling, S.J., Marine Historical Collection, University of Detroit Mercy.

Fig. 141: The *Ely* loads coal in Detroit around 1895. Courtesy of Fr. Edward J. Dowling, S.J., Marine Historical Collection, University of Detroit Mercy.

the sailboat as close as was possible to the derelict ship so that the sailors could jump off the rigging into the small boat. The men dropped into the sailboat four at a time, and the captain of the *Stone* towed them to shore. After repeating this heroic effort two more times, all eleven of the men were safe on shore, warming themselves by the fires.

The *Ely* was a total loss, valued at $12,500 at the time. Its three masts were removed, along with its sails, rigging, and tackle. Its deck machinery was left on board, since the ship was quite old by then. Apparently, no further attempts at salvage were made.

THE SHIPWRECK

Since the *Ely* shipwreck was located inside the harbor, it was not considered a hazard to navigation. The ship was never blown up or removed from the site of the sinking as a result. However, a new breakwater was built several years later on top of part of the wreck. This caused the stern of the ship to be buried under rock, so it has never been seen by scuba divers.

The sunken ship extends out from the breakwater at an angle toward shore. The *Ely* is still intact, with rocks

from a more recent breakwater improvement project holding the sides upright at the rear of the ship. The deck of the ship is still mostly intact, enabling divers to swim into the ship and out through the cargo hatch openings or through the open bow.

The bow has deteriorated considerably over the years. The forward part of the hull lies open, with the stem section lying on the rocky bottom next to the port side. It is not known how much damage occurred as a result of the sinking. A lot of damage may have been done by ships anchoring in that area of the harbor while waiting to load ore. Waves from storms have continually stressed the hull, causing the forward deck to disintegrate to an area behind the huge centerboard. Thick steel rods and plates installed by the GLSPS now stabilize the sides of the hull and reduce movement.

Several artifacts from the *Ely* shipwreck are on display in public places. These were removed by divers at earlier times and donated to local historical groups for all to see and enjoy. You may view these at the Two Harbors Lighthouse Museum, Lake Superior Maritime Visitor Center (Lakewalk) at Canal Park in Duluth, and in the *SS Meteor* Whaleback Ship Museum on Barker's Island in Superior, Wisconsin.

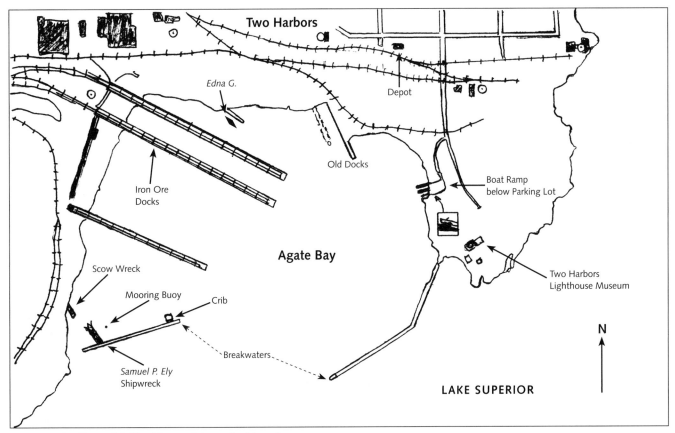

Map 15: The *Samuel P. Ely* shipwreck is marked by a buoy. Drawn by Stephen B. Daniel.

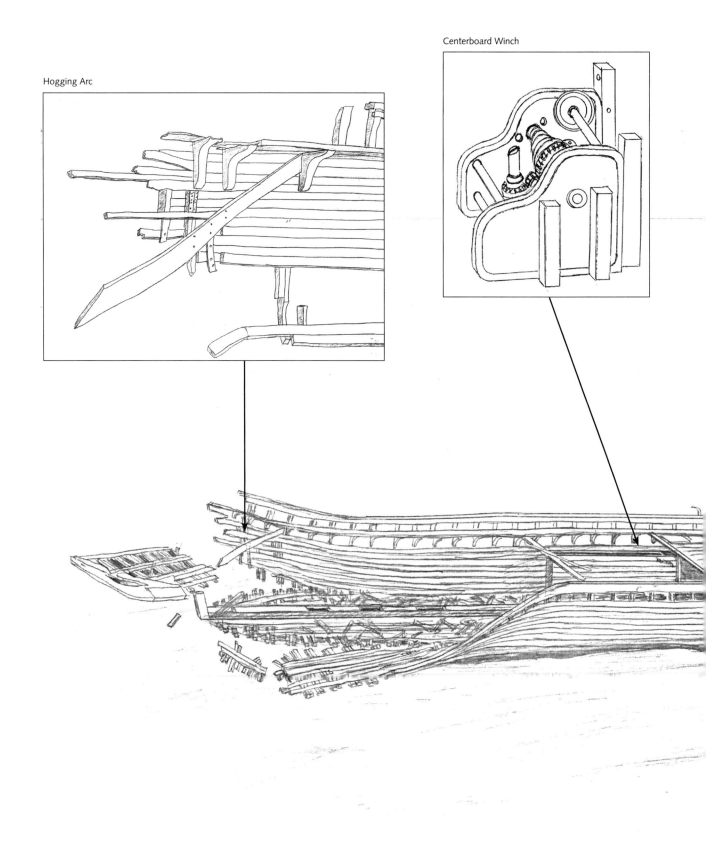

Hogging Arc

Centerboard Winch

Bollards

Belaying Pin Rack

Bilge Pump

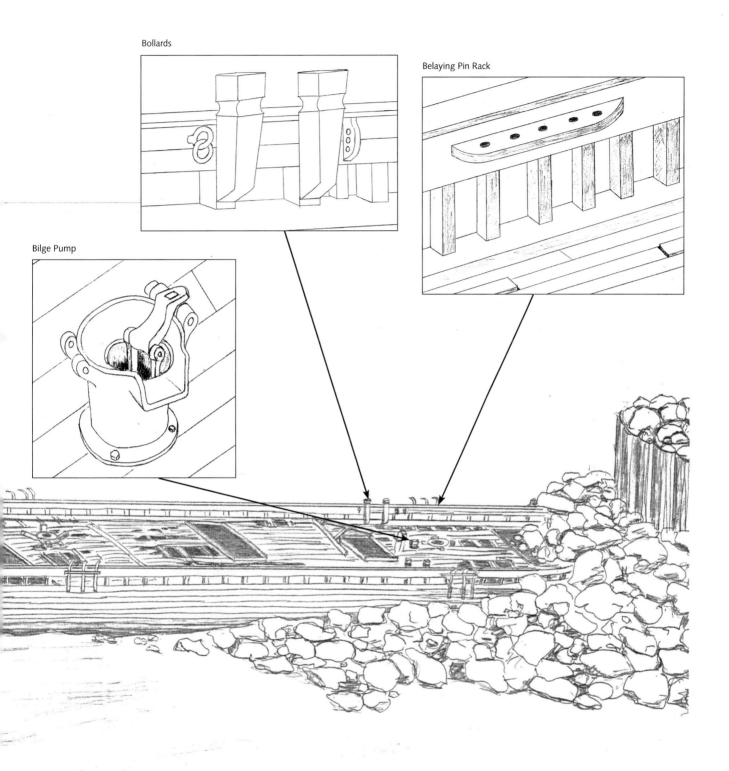

In July 2001, the GLSPS installed a shipwreck mooring buoy next to the *Ely* shipwreck. The mooring buoy is located about forty feet from the starboard side of the shipwreck. It will help preserve the ship by enabling dive boats to avoid placing anchors in the wreck. The buoy is placed on the shipwreck in the spring and removed in the fall.

DIVING THE *SAMUEL P. ELY*

Type of Vessel	Wooden schooner barge
Location	Next to west breakwater, across Agate Bay from Two Harbors Lighthouse Park near the ore docks
GPS Coordinates	47°00.699' N, 91°40.684' W
Depth	30 feet
Dive Rating	Intermediate diver

This dive is accessible by boat only. The closest launch site is the public boat ramp in the park near the Two Harbors lighthouse. When launching your boat, use caution to avoid rocks that are in shallow water on the outside of each of the docks. Use the mooring buoy or the breakwater to secure your boat, rather than anchoring near the shipwreck to avoid damaging the wood structure of the wreck. Post a lookout for other boats that may come into the area, and make certain to show a divers-down flag.

This shipwreck is relatively open and easy to penetrate. The open sections of the bow, missing deck sections, and cargo hatch openings allow good egress. Visibility is usually about fifteen to twenty-five feet but can be limited at times, since large ore freighters may stir up sediment on the bottom when they maneuver near the ore docks. Remember to use proper buoyancy control

to avoid touching the ship and stirring up silt inside the hull. The *Ely* shipwreck is protected, since it is listed on the National Register of Historic Places.

Fig. 144: Posts once held the belaying pin rail around the mast hole. Photo by Tamara Thomsen.

Fig. 145: The hatch combing around the cargo hatch is in good condition. Photo by Tamara Thomsen.

Fig. 143: Two Harbors boat ramp. Photo by Stephen B. Daniel.

Fig. 146: Side rails extend along the top of the hull on each side of the ship. Photo by Tamara Thomsen.

Fig. 147: Interesting forms may be found among pieces of wreckage. Photo by Tamara Thomsen.

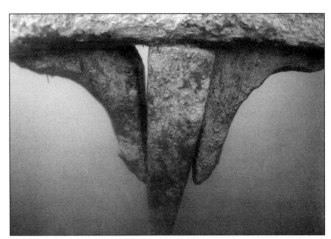

Fig. 148: The post and knees support the main deck of the *Ely*. Photo by Tamara Thomsen.

Preserving the *Samuel P. Ely*

The Great Lakes Shipwreck Preservation Society (GLSPS) was formed by a group of people who were alarmed at the rate of deterioration of this important example of lake schooners. A project to improve the breakwater in the late 1990s caused the deck to collapse into the hull. The GLSPS worked with the Minnesota Historical Society, the U.S. Army Corps of Engineers, and historical groups to develop a way to return the deck to its proper position. (See figs. 151–154, p. 72.)

The crew met on the ice in March 1996 to drill holes and lift the deck with cables suspended from winches on tripods. Divers went underneath the ice and drilled holes in the thick oak sides of the ship. Three-quarter-inch steel rods with turnbuckles were inserted into the holes and tightened with large nuts over one-half-inch thick steel plates on the outside of the hull. When the hull was secure, the deck was lowered back into place on the original ledges that were supposed to support it. In 2000 I was part of another GLSPS crew that replaced the first set of rods with one-inch steel rods and two turnbuckles to better handle the stresses of wave action the ship experiences underwater. It is hoped that these efforts will help the ship survive many more years underwater for the enjoyment of divers and historians alike.

Fig. 149 (left): The capstan from the *Ely* was once located on the forward deck near the bow. The bow came apart, probably dropping the capstan into the bilge area. Divers recovered the capstan and donated it to the Canal Park Lakewalk in Duluth, where it can be seen today. Push rods were inserted into the square holes at the top of the capstan to enable the crew to turn it and haul in the anchor chain and anchor. Photo by Stephen B. Daniel.

Fig. 150 (right): The ship's bell was recovered by divers and donated to the Two Harbors Lighthouse Museum. It is on display in the small white keeper's cottage next to the lighthouse. Photo by Stephen B. Daniel.

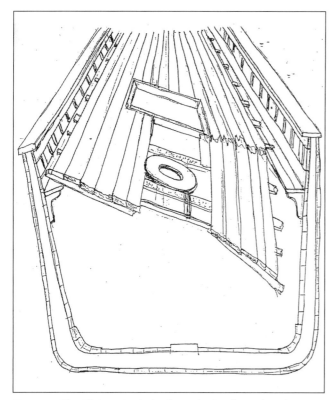

Fig. 151: The *Ely*'s main deck after it had collapsed at the stern. Drawing by Ken Merryman, Fridley, Minnesota.

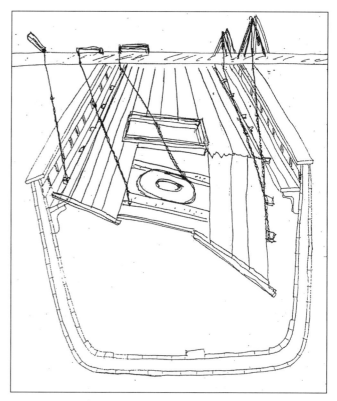

Fig. 152: Tripods were used to raise the deck. Drawing by Ken Merryman, Fridley, Minnesota.

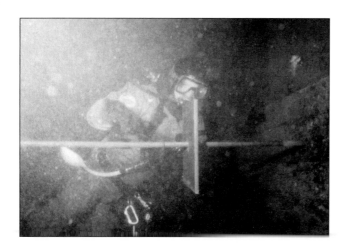

Fig. 153 (left): A diver inserts a steel rod with backing plate. Photo by Ken Merryman, Fridley, Minnesota.

Fig. 154 (left, below): A diver drills holes in the side of the hull. Photo by Ken Merryman, Fridley, Minnesota.

Fig. 155 (below): The sheet winch and bilge pump are on display at the *SS Meteor* Whaleback Ship Museum on Barker's Island in Superior, Wisconsin. Photo by Stephen B. Daniel.

Mooring Buoy near the *Ely*

The Great Lakes Shipwreck Preservation Society (GLSPS) installed a shipwreck mooring buoy next to the *Samuel P. Ely* shipwreck in July 2001. Holes were drilled in the rock bottom to bolt down anchor plates that held chains. A polypropylene line was secured to the chain and the lower end of the mooring buoy to hold it securely in place. A second mooring line was attached to the buoy for dive boats to use.

The mooring buoy is located about forty feet from the starboard side of the shipwreck. It will help preserve the ship by enabling dive boats to avoid placing anchors in the wreck. The buoy is placed on the shipwreck in the spring and removed in the fall by local GLSPS members, who continue to monitor the site to determine if more or other stabilizing systems are needed.

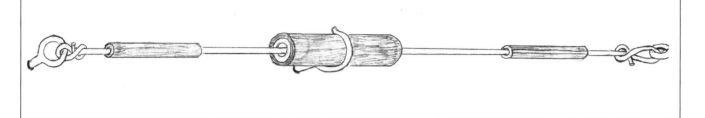

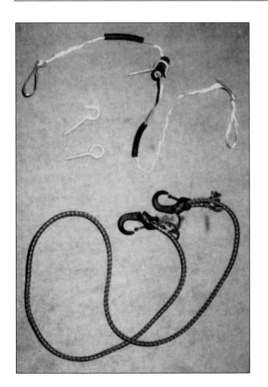

Fig. 156 (above): One end of the monitoring assembly is secured to an eyebolt that is fastened to a beam under the deck, and the opposite end is tied to the inside of the hull. Drawing by Stephen B. Daniel.

Fig. 157 (left): The *Ely* shipwreck is monitored annually to determine the amount of movement that the sides of the hull are experiencing over time. Polypropylene lines are threaded through rubber and plastic tubing sections and secured with a bowline on each end. The bungee cords help keep the lines taut. These simple devices record movement by moving the rubber sleeves on either side of the center sleeve. GLSPS members visit the wreck periodically to record the changes. Photo by Stephen B. Daniel.

Underwater Geology

Underwater Reef, Burlington Bay

Burlington Bay offers an opportunity for divers to do an easy shore dive. The dive site is located next to the Burlington Bay Campground, which has a boat ramp at its southeast edge. If you are not staying in the campground, check with the campground management regarding parking in the overflow lot across the street from the boat ramp.

Diving the Underwater Reef

Type of Structure	Reef and marine life
Location	Burlington Bay
Depth	12 feet
Dive Rating	Novice diver

Enter the water by the boat ramp, and swim toward a culvert. Then swim along the shoreline to view interesting rocky ledges that follow the side of the park underwater. The ledge continues out from shore as a reef. You may see trout, minnows, and bottom feeders, along with some discarded items, such as a shopping cart, that have made their way into the water. This also makes a good night dive. Caution should be used when following the reef, because it leads quite a distance into the lake. Be sure to use a divers-down flag.

Underwater Clay Formations, Flood Bay

Flood Bay was the site of some mining operations in the 1800s.[55] Railroad rails and mining artifacts, such as spikes, gears, axles, chains, and other metal parts may be found on the bottom. Remember to leave all artifacts where you find them. Fairly close to shore are interesting

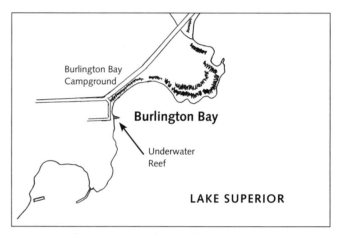

Map 16: Burlington Bay on the North Shore. Drawn by Stephen B. Daniel.

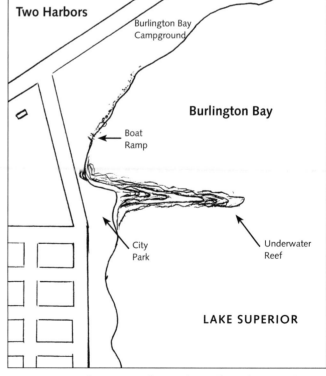

Map 17: An underwater reef extends out from shore on the point near the park. Drawn by Stephen B. Daniel.

74

clay formations along the bottom, in which the red clay seems to be squeezed out of black rock.

Fig. 158: **The path to the beach at Flood Bay.** Photo by Stephen B. Daniel.

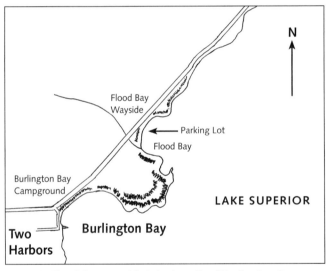

Map 18: Flood Bay wayside is just north of Burlington Bay Campgrounds. Drawn by Stephen B. Daniel.

DIVING FLOOD BAY

Type of Structure	Clay formations and steel and iron artifacts from old mining days
Location	About 1 mile north of Two Harbors
Depth	19 feet
Dive Rating	Novice diver

Turn off Highway 61 into the Flood Bay wayside rest area. Ample parking is available. An outhouse restroom is available a short distance from the parking lot for changing clothes. The large rocks around the parking lot may serve as a picnic surface. The wayside is also a nice

area for nondivers to enjoy the lake while divers are below.

This is a convenient dive site, with a short walk down a few steps to the beach. The depth is around nineteen feet, with visibility of twenty feet. Entry into the water from the beach is conveniently close to the parking lot.

Divers may come across rails and other artifacts from the early days of mining on the North Shore.

Sea Cave, Silver Creek

Sea caves have been formed by wave action on the cliffs at a few places along the North Shore. Silver Creek has one of these caves. It is located slightly southwest of the Silver Creek Cliff, which may be identified on shore by the stone nameplate "Silver Creek Tunnel" at the southwest end of the tunnel on Highway 61. The land immediately above the sea cave is privately owned and not accessible. Therefore, this is a boat dive. Divers may launch a boat at Two Harbors.

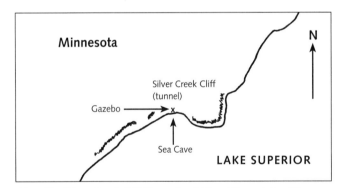

Map 19: Silver Creek Cliff is north of Flood Bay, at the Silver Creek Tunnel. Drawn by Stephen B. Daniel.

DIVING THE SEA CAVE

Type of Structure	Cave formed by waves hitting the cliff
Location	Slightly southwest of the Silver Creek Tunnel entrance
Depth	25 feet
Dive Rating	Novice diver

The sea cave is directly below a gazebo. The cave has a submerged arch that is about eight feet high, ten feet wide, and forty feet long.[56] When you pass through the arch, you will be able to see light at the other end of the cave. Visibility can be good enough for taking underwater photographs.

Shipwreck in Lake Superior at Encampment Island

Lafayette, Lafayette Bluff

The *Lafayette* was a steel bulk freighter built by the American Ship Building Company. The ship was launched on May 31, 1900, at Loraine, Ohio. The huge freighter was 454 feet long, with a beam of 50 feet, and a hold depth of 28 feet 5 inches; it grossed 5,113 tons.[57] The steam engine was capable of 1,800 horsepower. This was one of the first ships built by the Pittsburgh Steamship Company to carry iron ore from the North Shore to steel mills located along the shores of the lower Great Lakes.[58]

The steamer *Lafayette* cost $300,000 to build and was part of the "College Line," a group of five identical

Fig. 160: The *Lafayette* under way on Lake Superior. Courtesy of C. Patrick Labadie Collection, Superior, Wisconsin.

Fig. 159: The *Lafayette* about 1901–1904, in Conneaut, Ohio. Courtesy of Fr. Edward J. Dowling, S.J., Marine Historical Collection, University of Detroit Mercy.

vessels that were painted red on the hull, white on the cabins, and black on the smokestacks. A large white P was painted on the smokestack to identify the ship as part of the Pittsburgh Steamship fleet.[59]

The *Lafayette* was only five years old when it met its fate on Lake Superior late one night during a fierce November gale.

THE SINKING

On November 28, 1905, the *Lafayette* was steaming toward Duluth with its barge, the 436-foot, 5,039-ton *Manila*, in tow.[60] The ships were fighting terrific seas blown in from the northeast. One of the surging waves caused the *Manila* to ram the steamer, rendering the *Lafayette* helpless in the storm. Both of the big ships were slammed broadside into shore near a bluff near the north end of Encampment Island, six miles north of Two Harbors.

The bow of the *Lafayette* was more exposed to the storm near the point, so it took more of a beating by the waves. The forward section was battered to pieces, leaving only the stern section partially intact. Fortunately,

the crew on the bow section managed to jump to shore near a cliff where the ship came to rest. The rest of the ship's crew gathered together on the stern section when the ship broke apart. The ship's chief engineer threw a line to the crewmen on shore, who fastened it to a tree so the others could use it to reach safety. Only one

Fig. 162: Smashed bow section of the *Lafayette* next to the rocky shoreline north of Encampment Island. Courtesy of Lake Superior Maritime Collection, University of Wisconsin–Superior.

Fig. 161: The wreck of the *Lafayette* and the barge *Manila* on shore after the storm. Courtesy of C. Patrick Labadie Collection, Superior, Wisconsin.

Fig. 163: Tugs guide the stern section of the wrecked *Lafayette* through the Duluth Ship Canal toward salvage. Photo by Hugh McKenzie, courtesy of Kenneth E. Thro Collection, University of Wisconsin–Superior.

Fig. 164: Stern section of the wrecked *Lafayette*, with the barge *Manila* behind. Courtesy of Judge William Scott Collection, Lake County Historical Society, Two Harbors, Minnesota.

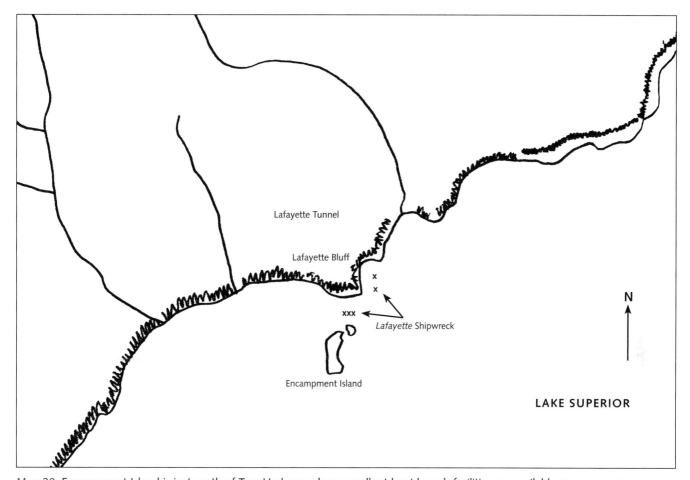

Map 20: Encampment Island is just north of Two Harbors, where excellent boat launch facilities are available. Drawn by Stephen B. Daniel.

sailor perished as a result of this horrible night. The bluff where the *Lafayette* wrecked was later named after the ship.

The *Manila* fared much better during the night, having been pushed into a more protected area along shore. The barge was later pulled free and repaired, and it then continued to carry cargo. The stern section of the *Lafayette* was all that remained of the big ship. It was towed to Duluth, where the engine was salvaged and the rest scrapped. The engine of the ship was later installed in a new steamer, the *J. S. Ashley*.[61]

THE SHIPWRECK

No intact sections of the steamer *Lafayette* remain, since 150 feet of the stern section was salvaged. However, there are many small pieces of wreckage that may be observed lying on the rocky bottom just off shore. Among the debris are some ceramic tiles, which may or may not be from the ship.

DIVING THE *LAFAYETTE*

Type of Vessel	Steel bulk freighter
Location	Next to shore at Lafayette Bluff, just north of Encampment Island
GPS Coordinates	47°05.695' N, 91°32.961' W
Depth	10–20 feet
Dive Rating	Novice diver

Private homes line the shore, and the only possible shore access would be down a steep slope about fifty yards northeast of the shipwreck site. So this shipwreck is most readily reached by boat. Depending on the weather, it may be best to anchor off shore to the east of the wreck site. The depth in this area is about fifty feet. Divers may swim from a boat toward shore by the point nearest the north side of Encampment Island. A reef extends from the point to the island. Swim over the reef, where debris will start to appear in ten to twenty feet of water. Follow the shoreline to view the debris field.

Small pieces of steel wreckage with beams attached may be found, along with small doors, brass fittings, and a copper pulley. Many other parts that have interesting

shapes and perforations may be seen on the bottom. This shallow dive may be an interesting second dive after a deeper adventure elsewhere.

The Return of an Artifact

The Great Lakes Shipwreck Preservation Society (GLSPS) will occasionally be contacted about returning artifacts to a shipwreck site or related museum; its Put-It-Back Committee helps facilitate this process. In 2000, Robert Anttila worked with the committee to return a solid brass binnacle stand once used to support a compass binnacle on the *Lafayette*. Anttila had recovered the artifact in 1955 during a dive with fellow members of the Frigid Frogs. He crafted a wood case to protect the binnacle stand during its travels from his home in California to Minnesota.

The GLSPS committee made arrangements with the Minnesota Historical Society to accept the artifact and provide it on loan to the Two Harbors Lighthouse Museum. The St. Louis County Historical Society had recently received funding from the Coastal Management Program for a shipwreck display at the museum. The informal transfer was completed on July 13, 2000, and the binnacle stand has been on display ever since.

Figs. 165–166: Robert Anttila donated the solid brass binnacle stand from the *Lafayette*. Photos by Stephen B. Daniel.

Ship Gone Missing in Lake Superior near Encampment Island

Lotta Bernard

The *Lotta Bernard* was built in 1869 as a sidewheel package and bulk freight steamer at Port Clinton, Ohio. The ship was 125 feet long and grossed 190 tons. After its launch it was fitted out in Sandusky, Ohio. The design of the ship—placing all the cabins in the rear—is an example of the "rabbit" type of steamer.[62] The sidewheel propulsion was very slow, producing a speed of four miles per hour. Critics said that the ship would have problems in heavy seas. Their prediction was to come true, as the *Bernard* experienced difficulty several times during storms on Lake Superior.

The *Lotta Bernard* was named after the daughter of the owner's partner and the owner's son. The open forward deck enabled the ship to conveniently haul cargoes of lumber, timber, and stone, as well as general freight, on the western end of Lake Superior. Its shallow draft enabled it to easily enter many ports on the north and south shores of the lake.[63]

The Sinking

The slow ship steamed from Thunder Bay to Duluth in late October 1874, when it encountered a storm. As the *Lotta Bernard* approached Encampment Island, it was wallowing in heavy seas, taking water over the stern. The huge waves smashed the cabins apart, until the smokestack was the only structure left standing. The captain ordered the pumps started to try to empty the water flowing into the decks below. The crew members valiantly stood by their posts, fighting to keep the ship afloat.

The captain ordered the bow anchor dropped, to swing the ship around to face into the seas, but the ship continued to take on water. This dire situation prompted

Fig. 165: The *Lotta Bernard*. Courtesy of Lake Superior Maritime Collection, University of Wisconsin–Superior.

the captain to order the two lifeboats launched so that the crew of thirteen and two passengers could safely escape from the sinking vessel. One of the lifeboats, which contained eight people, capsized when it was swamped by a huge wave while still by the side of the ship. Six people made it back to the remaining boat, but two drowned as they tried to hang on to the small capsized boat. The remaining lifeboat, though larger, was overloaded, since it already had seven on board. The storm turned into a blinding blizzard as darkness enveloped them. Several of the survivors tried to row the lifeboat in the fierce storm while the others bailed frantically to keep them afloat. They made their way slowly to the mainland near Silver Creek, just southwest of Encampment Island.

The captain then split the group in two to find help and shelter, since everyone was soaked through and very cold. The group of ten found a hospitable Indian camp, where they were given food and shelter and a chance to dry their clothes. The other group of three found the second lifeboat washed ashore and saw that it was in good shape. Ultimately, one of that group succumbed to exposure.[64]

After the storm subsided, the remaining twelve survivors returned to the two lifeboats and started to row toward Duluth. They encountered a small friendly fishing camp at Agate Bay (Two Harbors) and received food and an opportunity to get warm. Afterward, they continued to row another thirty-three miles to Duluth. This was a formidable feat, particularly at that time of year. The group arrived safely.

When the *Bernard* sank, it took a horse, two hundred sacks of flour, and sixty kegs of fish to the bottom with it. The ship was worth $20,000 at the time of the loss, but was insured only for $10,000.

The wreck of the *Lotta Bernard* has never been found.

Historic Artifacts in Lake Superior at Gooseberry River

Logging Camp

During the early part of the twentieth century, a logging camp was operating at the mouth of the Gooseberry River. Logging trains would bring carloads of timber from the north woods in the surrounding area to be moved to saw mills on the water. Today you can still see some rails in the open area of the mouth of the river, beyond where the river narrows.

Fig. 168: Several iron rails are visible in the water to the northeast of the river mouth. Photo by Stephen B. Daniel.

Belle P. Cross

The *Belle P. Cross* was built at a shipyard in Trenton, Michigan, and launched in 1870.[65] (It was rebuilt after a fire in 1901.) Owned by the Clow and Nicholson Transportation Company of Duluth, the wooden lumber hooker was 153 feet long and grossed 198 tons; it serviced logging operations along the North Shore. The *Cross* was a frequent caller at the Knife River and Gooseberry River logging camps.

On April 29, 1903, the *Cross* was carrying a load of railroad ties and timber on its way to Duluth from Two Islands (now Taconite Harbor). The ship encountered a blizzard that increased in intensity. The crew had difficulty seeing where they were because the storm hid the shore from view. Just south of the Gooseberry River

Fig. 169: The *Belle P. Cross* in Buffalo, New York, around 1882. Courtesy of Port Huron Museum, Port Huron, Michigan.

Fig. 170: The *Belle P. Cross* about 1900 at Grand Marais, Minnesota. Courtesy of C. Patrick Labadie Collection, Superior, Wisconsin.

DIVING THE GOOSEBERRY RIVER LOGGING ARTIFACTS

Type of Artifacts	Railroad rails and steam fittings, *Belle P. Cross* rudder
Location	Northeast side of the river mouth and along cliffs on the southeast side
Depth	20 feet; 55 feet (rudder)
Dive Rating	Novice diver

the *Cross* struck the reef hard at Castle Danger. The crew abandoned the ship and headed for shore a short distance away. The waves that were rolling toward shore started to tear the ship apart. The *Cross* and its cargo were battered to pieces.

The engine, boilers, pumps, anchors, and chains were recovered by salvors right after the wreck. The stranding on the reef at Castle Danger resulted in a $12,000 loss of the ship.[66] Only the rudder has been located by divers to date. No other evidence of the shipwreck has been found underwater in the area.

There are also some sea caverns that may be visited underwater along the south side of the low cliffs. The depth here can be as much as twenty feet next to the cliffs, depending on lake levels.

A Minnesota State Park sticker is required to enter the Gooseberry Falls State Park. To access the dive sites, drive through the park toward the end of the road past the campgrounds. A parking lot is located near a path leading to the stony beach. A restroom sign marks the path. Picnic tables are usually available nearby for gearing up.

Both dive sites may be accessed from the stony beach; the cliffs are closest to the south end of the beach. The artifacts are strewn among the rocks on the bottom. Do not remove any artifacts from the site: they belong to the State of Minnesota and are best preserved in the water for other divers to see. The railroad rails may be seen by swimming north across the river mouth. Avoid the dark turbulent water in the narrow area of the mouth of the river. The *Belle P. Cross* rudder is located seventy-five feet out from shore where the rock gradually drops into the water, at a fifty-five-foot depth.

Fig. 171: Many large metal logging artifacts may be observed along the base of these cliffs. In the background is the beach that may be used for access to the dive site. Photo by Stephen B. Daniel.

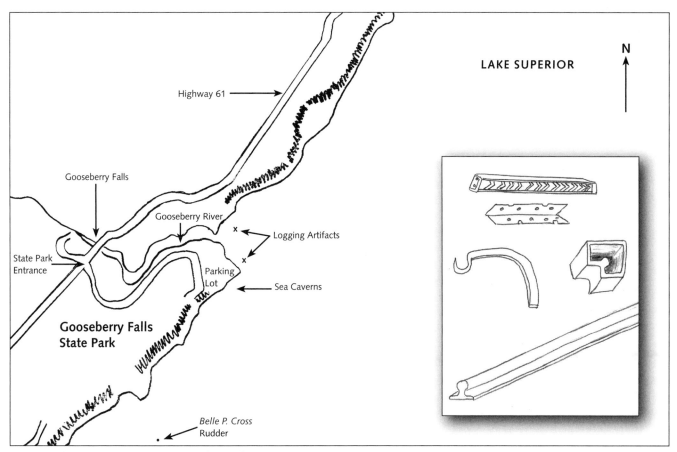

Map 21: The *Belle P. Cross* rudder is offshore from Gooseberry Falls State Park. Drawn by Stephen B. Daniel. Fig. 172 (inset): Logging artifacts are located on both sides of the Gooseberry River mouth. Drawing by Stephen B. Daniel.

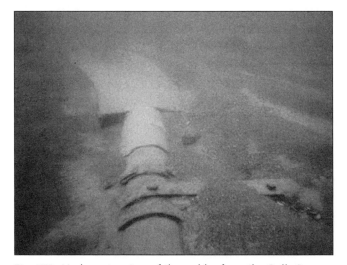

Fig. 173: Underwater view of the rudder from the *Belle P. Cross* along shore, southeast of the Gooseberry River. Courtesy of Elmer Engman, Proctor, Minnesota.

Fig. 174: A restroom sign marks the path leading to the stony beach that serves as an entry point for the logging artifact dive. Photo by Stephen B. Daniel.

Historic Artifacts in Lake Superior at Split Rock Island

Criss Grover

The *Criss Grover* was a merchant schooner built and launched at Lorraine, Ohio, in 1878. The ship was ninety feet long and grossed 133 tons. Its home port for several years was Marquette, Michigan, under the master of Captain Daniels.[67] The *Grover* transported dynamite to mining towns around Lake Superior, a task many ship masters chose to avoid. The ship sank in Marquette Harbor in 1889 and was repaired afterward by Captain Gibson.

While sailing from Bay Mills, Michigan, to Duluth in October 1899, the schooner was caught in a gale and driven onto a reef near Split Rock Island. It broke up in the storm and was a total loss. The captain probably ordered the anchor to be cast overboard in a last ditch attempt to save his ship. It caught hard in the rocks, but the anchor line may have snapped. The anchor remains securely in place, where it can be seen by divers.

DIVING THE CRISS GROVER

Type of Artifacts	Schooner anchor and hull section from *Criss Grover*
Location	Northeast side of Split Rock Island and southwest side of island, respectively
Depth	53 feet
Dive Rating	Novice diver

Fig. 175: The boat ramp at Sve's (accessible off Highway 61) is available for small boats for a nominal launch fee. Split Rock Island is visible in the background. Photo by Stephen B. Daniel.

This dive site is best reached by boat. The Sve Boat Launch off Highway 61, north of the bridge over the Split Rock River, is most convenient for small boats, such as a Zodiac. Larger craft may be launched at the Twin Points Boat Ramp, just south of Sve. The nine-foot schooner anchor is located east of the island, wedged firmly in

rocks in about fifty-three feet of water. A section of the hull with a porthole opening is located on the bottom by the edge of the reef plateau on the southwest side of the island. Square nails, in various sizes, may be found at the north end of the split between the islands in shallow water (three to four feet deep).

Fig. 176 (right): Anchor in the rocks by Split Rock Island, believed to be from the *Criss Grover*. Courtesy of Andrew Leidel, Minneapolis, Minnesota.

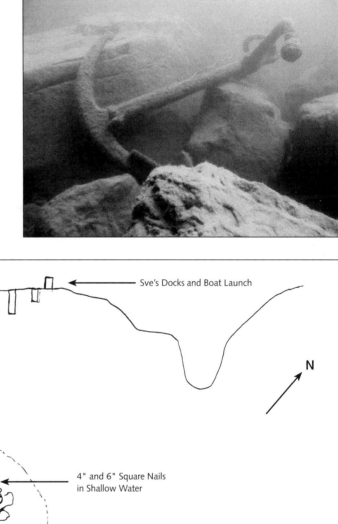

Fig. 177 (below): Ship hull section with porthole opening. Drawn by Stephen B. Daniel.

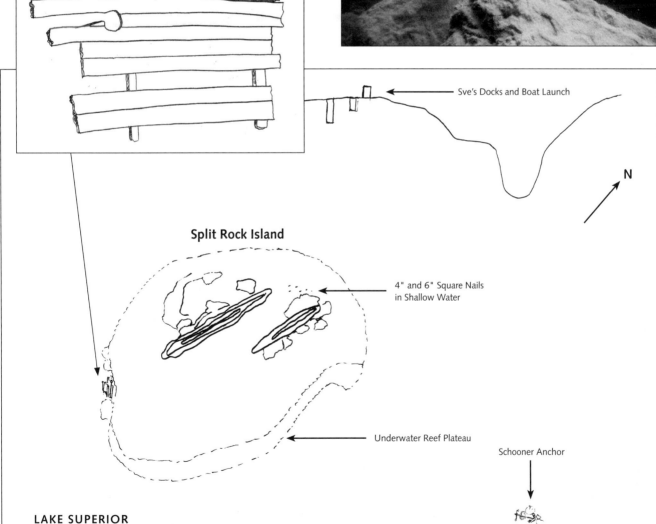

Sve's Docks and Boat Launch

N

Split Rock Island

4" and 6" Square Nails in Shallow Water

Underwater Reef Plateau

Schooner Anchor

LAKE SUPERIOR

Map 22: Split Rock Island and nearby wreckage. Drawn by Stephen B. Daniel.

Fig. 178: The Twin Points Boat Ramp is located south of Split Rock Island. Photo by Stephen B. Daniel.

Fig. 179: View of Split Rock Island, with Sve's on the mainland in the background. The anchor is to the right, and the section of the ship's side is to the left. Photo by Stephen B. Daniel.

Historic Artifacts in Lake Superior at Split Rock River

Logging Dam

A large logging settlement was operated by the Split Rock Lumber Company at the mouth of the Split Rock River in the early part of the twentieth century. The camp had about 50 employees, while another 350 men worked back in the woods harvesting tall stands of red and white pines. Three locomotives would bring strings of railcars loaded with logs to the river mouth. A dam was built across the mouth to raise the water level, forming a pond behind the dam. The log pilings and timber construction of the dam were sturdy and held the logs after the trains dumped them into the pond.[68]

A wharf 184 feet long and 16 feet wide was built on cribs filled with rocks. It extended out from shore into 14 feet of water. The wharf was used by steamers and freighters bringing supplies and transporting the logs to the sawmills.

Fig. 180: The tug *Gladiator* was operated near the mouth of the Split Rock River by Merrill & Ring. The big tug was used to tow log booms assembled by the Split Rock Lumber Company to the sawmill in Duluth. Courtesy of Northeast Minnesota Historical Center.

Fig. 181: Headquarters of the Split Rock Lumber Company near the Split Rock River. Courtesy of Northeast Minnesota Historical Center.

Fig. 182: Logging dam ruins at the mouth of Split Rock River. Photo by Stephen B. Daniel.

Fig. 183: Pilings once supported a structure across the mouth of the river so that logs could be floated down to the lake. Photo by Stephen B. Daniel.

The Split Rock and Northern Railroad, operated by the logging company, terminated its ten-mile track from the woods at the river mouth. The Split Rock Lumber Company had a coal dock and store on a site adjacent to the small harbor. A warehouse, post office, two dormitories, and a dining room were located nearby. An ice house and seven homes completed the small settlement.

When the weather was nice, the trains would dump the logs directly into the lake from a trestle that ran along the shoreline. Large rafts of logs would be assembled using log booms and chains to form a bag-like formation that could be towed by a tug. The logs were towed to sawmills in Duluth, where the logs were cut into lumber. About fifty million logs were towed away each year in the rafts, according to a 1903 U.S. Army Corps of Engineers report.[69]

The remains of the logging dam on the northeast shore and the pilings extending across the river mouth into the bay are all that is left of the logging camp. The pilings provide an interesting shallow dive for viewing part of the history of the North Shore. The site attracts shore visitors and anglers, who enjoy basking in the sun while sitting on the sand bar waiting for fish to bite.

The *William Edenborn* was blown aground at this site in a gale on November 28, 1905 (see p. 100). The heavily damaged steam freighter was recovered but eventually was sunk intentionally near Cleveland, Ohio, where it serves as a breakwater.

DIVING THE SPLIT ROCK RIVER LOGGING DAM

Type of Artifacts	Pilings from the log boom dam
Location	River mouth on east side of Highway 61
Depth	15 feet
Dive	Novice diver

You can reach the dive site from shore by parking on the side of the old road, off the Gitchi-Gami State Trail. Dive

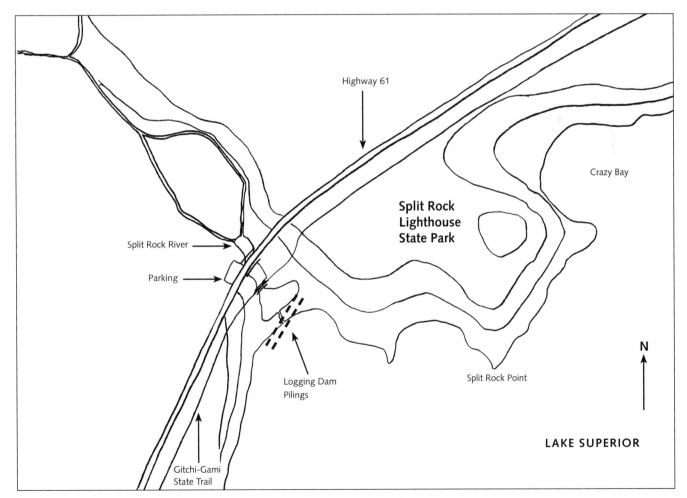

Map 23: Pilings remaining from the logging dam rest at the mouth of the Split Rock River. Drawn by Stephen B. Daniel, based on Split Rock Lighthouse State Park map from the Minnesota Department of Natural Resources.

gear may be hauled along the gravel bike trail; you may find a wagon with balloon tires helpful.

Signs along the path caution against taking a shortcut that could harm vegetation. Wide stone steps just before the bridge allow convenient access down the hillside to the sandy beach at the edge of the river.

This dive site may also be reached by boat. The Twin Points Boat Ramp is located south of the river off Highway 61. It is a pleasant boat ride to the Split Rock River mouth.

The best time to do this shallow dive is after a dry spell, which often happens in August, when the river is low and suspended sediment is at a minimum; visibility is generally poor. The logging dam begins on the northeast side of the river mouth and extends across the river mouth, and pilings from the logging dam continue across the sand bar and into the bay. Some additional pilings are located in about fifteen feet of water, out from the row of pilings that formed the logging dam. These may be from the wharf that was built for the ships to dock here.

Fig. 184: Steps to the beach near the log dam pilings. Photo by Stephen B. Daniel.

The bays to the northeast of the river mouth have been reported to contain a donkey boiler and some other metal artifacts on the bottom. These are likely discarded items from the logging camp operations.

Historic Artifacts in Lake Superior at Little Two Harbors

Fishing Village and *Madeira* Salvage

Little Two Harbors is located within Split Rock Lighthouse State Park (a state park motor vehicle pass is required for entry). A small fishing village was once located at the edge of the protected bay formed by the island in the harbor. Later the land was sold to the Minnesota Department of Natural Resources, at which time it became part of the state park. The gravel beach section on the southwest side changes in size with wind and wave action.

During 1974 (before the area became a state park), a salvage operation was conducted by Lee Opheim, who had purchased the rights to the *Madeira* shipwreck (see pp. 99–111) from the Great Lakes Steel Corporation. He proceeded to remove loose parts of wreckage from the shipwreck site. The large pieces of metal were probably raised with a lift bag or other float device and towed to the beach on the southwest side of the little bay. The metal was then cut up with a welding torch in an attempt

Fig. 185 (above): The fishing village was located behind the person on shore at the right. Photo by Stephen B. Daniel.

Fig. 186 (left): Little Two Harbors Bay, where wreckage from the *Madeira* salvage operation may be seen underwater (just to the right of the island). Photo by Stephen B. Daniel.

to provide scrap metal for profit. The salvage operation turned out to be an unprofitable venture and was abandoned. The remaining wreckage was discarded in the bay.

Diving Little Two Harbors Artifacts

Type of Artifacts	Cribs from the docks of the fishing village, hull section from the *Madeira*, and other wreckage
Location	Split Rock State Park, near the picnic area by the campground
Depth	12 feet
Dive	Novice diver

Divers may easily reach this dive site from the pebble beach. The cribs from the fishing village are located out

from the shoreline on the west side of the bay. The wreckage from the *Madeira* salvage operation lies near the base of the rocky island on the south side of the bay, just north of the island, underwater. In addition to the large hull section, you may find long, narrow pipes (about two inches in diameter), a steel tire rim from a truck, and a large-diameter pipe. Some small steel plates are also resting on the bottom. The visibility is twenty feet.

Map 24 (below): A dive site with artifacts from the *Madeira* can be reached from the pebble beach at Split Rock State Park. Drawn by Stephen B. Daniel, based on Split Rock Lighthouse State Park map from the Minnesota Department of Natural Resources.

Fig. 187 (inset): Railroad rails at Split Rock Point. Drawing by Tidewater Atlantic Research, courtesy of Minnesota Historical Society / State Historic Preservation Office.

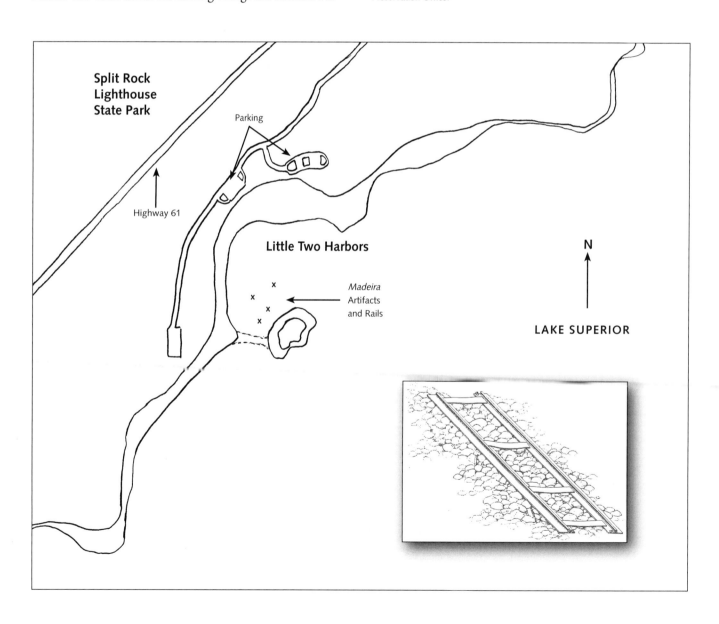

Fig. 188: Fishing village at Little Two Harbors. Remains of the cribs used for the docks may be seen underwater in the bay. Courtesy of the Minnesota Historical Society.

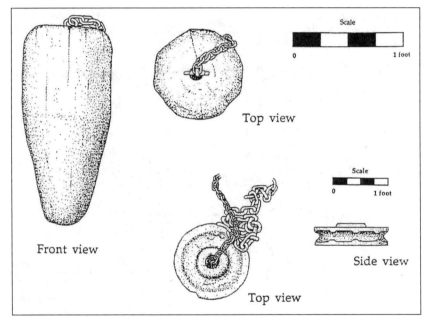

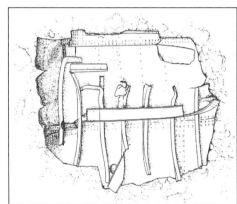

Fig. 189 (above): Section of the hull of the *Madeira*. Drawing by Tidewater Atlantic Research, courtesy of Minnesota Historical Society / State Historic Preservation Office.

Fig. 190 (above): Wooden buoy and weights discovered in the bay at Little Two Harbors during an underwater survey conducted by the Minnesota Historical Society in 1992. Drawing by Tidewater Atlantic Research, courtesy of Minnesota Historical Society / State Historic Preservation Office.

Fig. 191 (right): Little Two Harbors was used as a work site to cut up metal recovered from the *Madeira* shipwreck during salvage operations in 1974. Note the kedge anchor in the foreground. The gravel beach area on the mainland, on which the salvage metal pieces are resting, is mostly eroded by waves today. Courtesy of Richard Sve, Two Harbors, Minnesota.

Underwater Geology

PART 3

Boulder Field and Sea Caves, Split Rock Lighthouse

The Split Rock Lighthouse provides a picturesque view to boaters who cruise along the North Shore. A museum that includes a display and video on the *Madeira* shipwreck is located adjacent to the lighthouse. The shipwreck is located in the next bay to the north of the lighthouse, at the base of Gold Rock Point. (See pp. 99–111 for more on the *Madeira*.)

The lighthouse served an important function to mariners before radar, Loran C radio beacons, and satellite global positioning systems were invented. The common use of these newer technologies has replaced the need for the light and fog horns once operated by the lighthouse keepers. The lighthouse is still lit for special events.

The boulder field is composed of huge rocky structures; it looks as if a giant threw them into the lake from shore. The boulders are resting in piles, and some of them are the size of a small house. Several openings among the boulders provide an interesting "swim-through" for divers. You will be impressed by the size of the boulders as you swim over, around, and under them. The boulder field stops about a hundred feet off shore, leaving the flat sand and rock bottom to continue toward the lake.

A second interesting dive site is located at the base of the cliff, where a hoist on a concrete platform once operated. The small derrick was used to haul supplies up from ships waiting below to unload construction equipment and materials, which were used to build the lighthouse in the early 1900s. Occasionally, yellow bricks would fall overboard in the process, landing in the sand at the base of the cliff. Some of these may still be observed, but many have been taken by visiting divers in the past. Fortunately, the diving ethic today is to look at artifacts but leave them in place for other divers to see.

Fig. 192: The boulder field begins underwater on the starboard side of the sailboat. Sea caves are located below the hoist site, slightly northeast of the lighthouse. Photo by Stephen B. Daniel.

Two small caves have been formed at the base of this cliff, having been carved out by stormy seas over the ages. The depth at the caves is about twenty feet.

DIVING THE BOULDER FIELD AND SEA CAVES

Type of Structure	Huge boulders and rocks, shallow caves
Location	Below the lighthouse, offshore from the cliff at the southeast side
Depth	55 feet (boulder field); 20 feet (sea caves)
Dive	Novice diver

This is a boat dive. Boats may be launched at the Twin Points Boat Ramp, south of the lighthouse off Highway 61. A depth finder will help locate the pile of boulders that make up the boulder field. Make certain your anchor is set to secure the boat, and post a divers-down flag. (The Split Rock Lighthouse is a popular site for boaters to visit.)

The boulder field is located approximately a hundred feet from shore and extends out another hundred feet, at a depth of fifty-five feet.

The sea caves are located below the hoist platform at the top of the cliff on the northeast side of the lighthouse. The caves may be partially visible above the water, depending on lake levels. The depth of the caves at the sandy bottom is about twenty feet. You may easily swim into and out of the sea cave on the east side. The westerly sea cave appears to be blocked by some large boulders. Look for an opening between the boulders that will allow you to enter the cave. When the sun is out, it will provide some illumination. Exercise caution when attempting to enter the sea cave, as years of severe weather may change the access opening.

Fig. 194: Large boulders stand in front of sea caves at the base of the cliff under the old hoist site. Divers may swim through an opening to observe the interior, which is illuminated by sunlight. *Drawing by Stephen B. Daniel.*

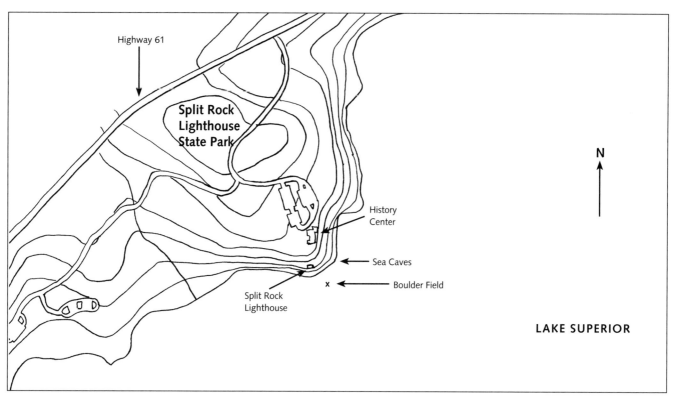

Map 25: Sea caves and a boulder field are part of a scenic dive near the Split Rock Lighthouse. Drawn by Stephen B. Daniel, based on Split Rock Lighthouse State Park map from the Minnesota Department of Natural Resources.

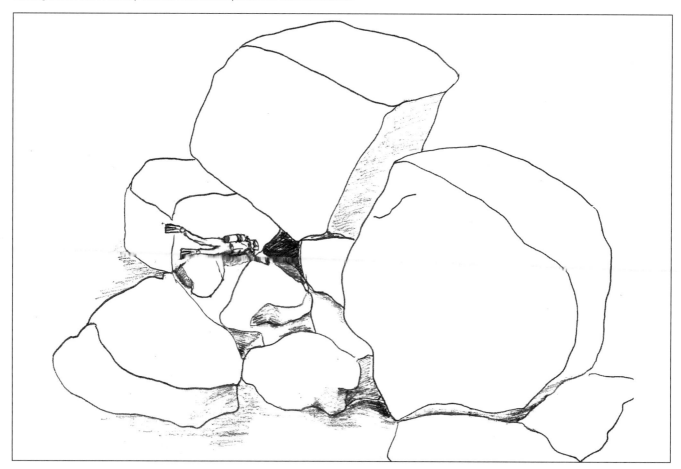

Fig. 194: Huge boulders, some the size of a small house, provide an interesting dive. Drawing by Stephen B. Daniel.

Shipwreck in Lake Superior at Gold Rock Point

Madeira

The *Madeira* was a steel schooner-barge built by the Chicago Shipbuilding Company and launched in South Chicago in 1900. The ship was 436 feet long and grossed 5.039 tons.[70] Its three masts with small sails were intended to help power it while being towed in open water.

The hull consisted of riveted heavy steel plates, and most of the superstructure of the ship was made of steel, with some wood joinery. There was no engine installed for propulsion, but a donkey boiler assisted with raising the anchors and handling the heavy lines. The ship was designed to carry bulk freight (typically grain and iron ore) on the Great Lakes, with a flat bottom to maximize cargo capacity, while drawing a minimum draft. The *Madeira* had two sister ships, built with a similar design: the *Marsala*, which was an exact duplicate, and the *Manila*, which ran aground during the same storm that caused the *Madeira* to wreck.[71]

The *Madeira* was originally owned by the Minnesota Steamship Company, which operated out of Cleveland, Ohio, from 1900 to 1901. The ship was then sold to the Pittsburgh Steamship Company, which also operated from Ohio. It ran into the International Bridge at Sault Ste. Marie in 1902.[72]

Fig. 195: Starboard side view of the *Madeira* c. 1900–1905. Courtesy of Historical Collections of the Great Lakes, Bowling Green State University, Ohio.

THE SINKING

On November 28, 1905, the *Madeira* was being towed by the 478-foot, 5,900-ton steel steamer *William Edenborn* down the lake toward Duluth. A fierce November gale had been building, which would become known as the *Mataafa* Storm, named after the shipwreck that blocked the Duluth Ship Canal as a result of the gale. Storm warnings had been raised on the western end of the lake beginning on November 23. The powerful 1,800-horsepower engine of the *Edenborn* could not control the heavy steel barge in tow while it was pitching in the high seas.

The two ships had difficulty staying on course as the storm raged on. Snow and darkness eliminated all visibility, and the ships sailed dangerously close to shore. The tow line parted along the way, leaving the *Madeira* to drift on its own. Realizing they had lost their tow, the captain of the *Edenborn* decided to increase its speed to bring the ship into the wind so that it could drop anchor and ride out the storm in deeper water. He was disori-

ented by the snow and darkness, however, so instead of heading toward deeper water, the ship bore down on the mouth of the Split Rock River, grinding to a halt as it beached on the shore with the bow protruding into the woods. The storm and the ship's precarious position on the rocky shoreline caused it to break in half. The crew rushed into the forward cabins to seek shelter. One crewman lost his life when he fell into the hold through an open cargo hatch, after the hatch covers popped off as the ship settled. All the other *Edenborn* crew survived.[73]

Meanwhile, the *Madeira* was left foundering in the heavy seas as it drifted for two hours toward shore after the towline broke. The captain did not have any idea of their position, and the big barge suddenly crashed broadside into solid rock. The huge waves began to pound the ship against the cliff, causing it to break apart.

One of the seamen, Fred Benson, jumped from the ship as it rode up on a wave, grabbing a rocky outcrop and boosting himself up the sheer cliff. He climbed to the top and tied a line to a rock, throwing it back to the men

Fig. 196: Painting of the *Madeira* shipwreck by Kurt Carlson. Courtesy of Great Lakes Historical Society, Whitefish Point, Michigan.

trapped on the bow of the ship. He helped three more crewmen climb to safety. Benson then proceeded to throw his weighted line to the men on the stern section of the ship. A hawser line was attached, which he pulled back up and secured at the top of the cliff. Five more men climbed up and were saved. Only one crewman, Mate James Morrow, died when he climbed the mizzenmast and drowned, taken down with the sinking ship.[74]

The captain and crew made their way through deep snow to a fisherman's cabin, where they warmed up and dried off. They were picked up at Split Rock River by the tug *Edna G.* a few days later. The *Madeira* continued to break apart as waves pounded it against the cliff through the night. The shattered hull sank to the bottom along the base of the west side of Gold Rock Point. The 1905 storm caused tremendous loss of men, ships, and cargoes. The Split Rock Lighthouse was built on the neighboring cliff to the south in 1910, as a result of both shipping interests and the loss of the *Madeira*.

The Shipwreck

The *Madeira* remained untouched underwater for fifty years. In the summer of 1955 the Frigid Frogs, a Duluth diving club, discovered the *Madeira*. Much of what they found remains in place today. In fact, on a clear day, nondivers may be able to see portions of the sides of the ship and other debris in shallow water along the base of the cliff. The upended bow section is located closest to shore in 40 feet of water. The small portion of deck that is still attached faces toward the mainland. The port side of the ship is bent sharply and extends up the rocky slope toward the cliff.

The fantail stern section, remarkably intact, rests on its starboard side in 60 feet of water, about 110 feet toward the lake from the bow section. A section of the port hull side extends up the slope toward the cliff. The tiller is in place on deck, along with a windlass that was used for raising the stern anchor. Some bollards are still mounted on each side of the afterdeck. You can observe steering gear and chains by shining a light into the inside of the hull.

The pilothouse, which tends to move around with stormy seas, is farther along the bottom (about 80 to 100 feet into the lake) in about 85 feet of water. A mast, a pump, the smokestack, and other debris are strewn along the bottom to a 115-foot depth. Additional pieces of the ship are scattered among rocks on the slope toward the cliff. Some midship sections of the hull were found about

200 feet to the west of the stern section in about 100 feet of water by the Panamerican group that surveyed the wreck site.[75]

The Salvage Attempt

The title to the shipwreck was purchased from the Pittsburgh Steamship Division of United States Steel Corporation in July 1960 by the Schwalen-Opheim Corporation, based in Duluth. The group made several intermittent attempts to salvage parts of the *Madeira* over the next several years. The anchors were the most significant recovery; the bow anchor is displayed next to the site where the Split Rock Trading Post gift shop on Highway 61 once stood, next to the wayside rest stop. Bollards and a tangled piece of the steel hull were also

Fig. 197: Members of the Frigid Frogs, Dick Metz, Ed Langlois, Bruce Keeley, and Vince Jordan, pose with the wheel from the *Madeira*. Courtesy of Great Lakes Marine Collection, Milwaukee Public Library / Wisconsin Marine Historical Society.

Fig. 198: The wheel from the *Madeira* on display in the SS *Meteor* Whaleback Ship Museum on Barker's Island in Superior, Wisconsin. Photo by Stephen B. Daniel.

Salvaging the Bow Anchor

The anchors from the *Madeira* were sold as part of the salvage operation. Richard Hewitt and Ray Peterson removed the starboard bow anchor from the hawse hole after considerable effort. Once removed, the five-thousand-pound anchor was supported by two empty marine fuel barrels used as lift devices. One was attached to the anchor underwater; a come-along was used to winch the anchor and submerged barrel to the surface, where the other barrel floated. Ray used his boat to tow the anchor and barrels to Sve Landing near Split Rock Island. Ragnvald Sve helped bring the anchor on shore with his bulldozer, using large logs and a heavy chain to get it closer to the ramp. Two smaller logs were used as skids under the flukes. Ragnvald dragged the heavy load up the ramp and across the ground. Later, a wrecker truck with special rigging lifted the anchor into a dump truck, which Bill Matthies had arranged for. The anchor was hauled away for display in Brainerd and later found its way to its current location on the North Shore.

Figs. 199–201 (clockwise from above): Near a historical marker by Highway 61, the *Madeira*'s bow anchor, a piece of riveted hull, and bollards are on display. Photos by Stephen B. Daniel.

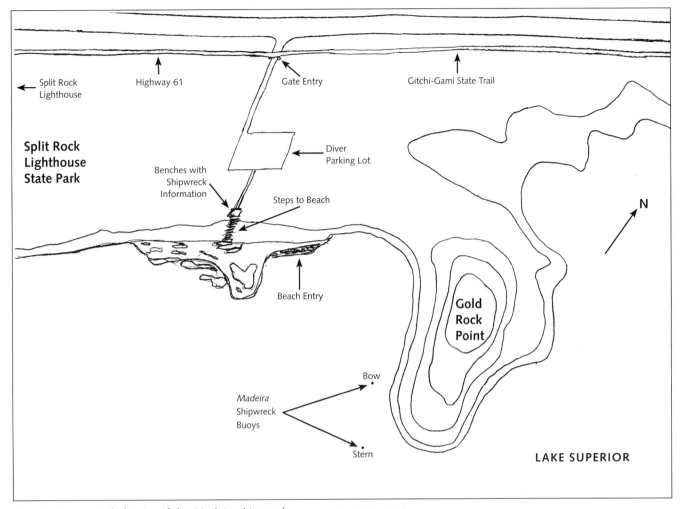

Map 26: Buoys mark the site of the *Madeira* shipwreck. Drawn by Stephen B. Daniel.

removed and may be seen near the bow anchor. The stern kedge anchor is located on the corner of Third Street and Vernon Street in West Duluth. One of the ship's wheels and the steam gauge were removed and displayed at the Split Rock Trading Post, but they were lost when the store burned down.

Many pieces of salvaged metal were removed from the debris area and transported to the bay at Little Two Harbors, southwest of the Split Rock Lighthouse. The salvors constructed a small, narrow rail line to move the heavy pieces of steel to a beach, where they cut them into smaller pieces using a welding torch. The metal was then sold for scrap. After 1974, the salvage attempt was abandoned. A large section of the hull side was dropped into the bay at Little Two Harbors. A few remaining metal pieces were also left on the bottom of the bay, along with pipes, a section of the rail line, and some other metal debris. These may be viewed underwater by divers who consider visiting Little Two Harbors.

DIVING THE *MADEIRA* SHIPWRECK

Type of Vessel	Steel schooner-barge
Location	At base of west side of Gold Rock Point
GPS Coordinates	47°12.360′ N, 91°21.480′ W
Depth	25–115 feet
Dive Rating	Advanced diver

The *Madeira* may be reached by swimming from the pebble beach on shore or from boats moored to one of the mooring buoys (installed each spring and removed each fall). A Minnesota State Park pass is required for entry to the gated parking lot off Highway 61. The code to the combination padlock on the gate is available from the ranger at the entrance to Split Rock State Park. You can launch a boat at Twin Points Boat Ramp, south off Highway 61. The first mooring buoy is attached to the bow section in 40 feet of water. The second mooring buoy is attached to the stern section in 60 feet of water. The pilothouse rests on the sand at an 80-foot depth, and the smokestack is by the edge of the cliff at 115 feet.

Some hull plates may be found in shallower water toward shore. The sides of the ship extend up the rock slope toward the cliff of Gold Rock Point to a depth of 10 feet. Pipes, pumps, and a mast may be found among the debris at various depths. Some items move around with storm action and may change location season to season. The *Madeira* shipwreck is protected, since it is listed on the National Register of Historic Places.

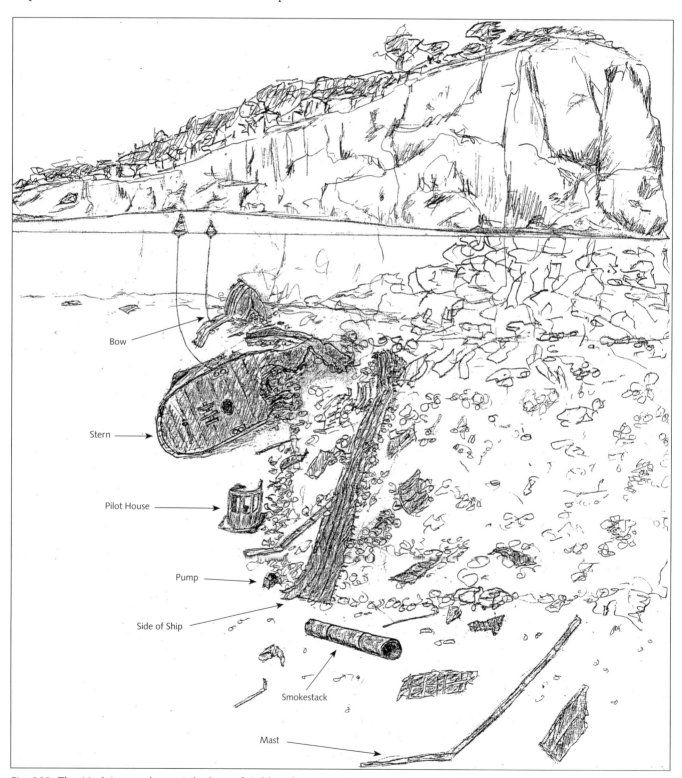

Fig. 202: The *Madeira* wreckage at the base of Gold Rock Point. *Drawing by Stephen B. Daniel.*

Fig. 203 (top): The bow section of the *Madeira* dwarfs the diver swimming alongside it. Photo by Tamara Thomsen.
Fig. 204 (bottom): A diver peers into a hatch on the stern deck. Photo by Tamara Thomsen.

Fig. 205 (top): Portholes may be observed in some sections of the hull. Photo by Tamara Thomsen.
Fig. 206 (bottom): The view of the wreckage from inside the broken hull section offers unusual perspective. Photo by Tamara Thomsen.

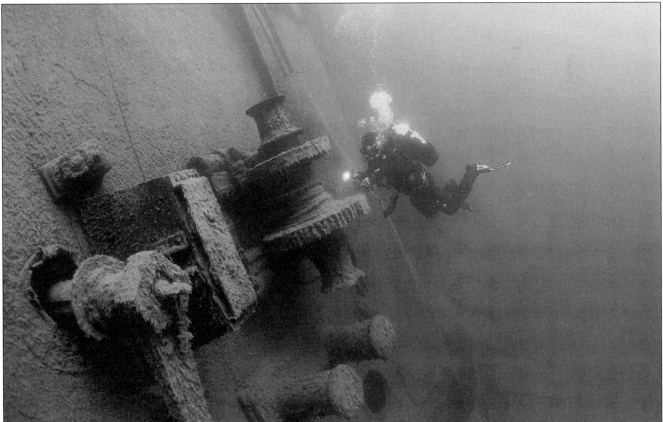

Fig. 207 (top): A diver examines the pilothouse. Photo by Tamara Thomsen.
Fig. 208 (bottom): The stern deck holds interesting machinery, such as the winch. Photo by Tamara Thomsen.

Fig. 209 (top): A diver views the hole in the bow section made during the salvage operation. Photo by Tamara Thomsen.
Fig. 210 (bottom): Steel frames once held the hull side to the bottom of the ship. Photo by Tamara Thomsen.

Fig. 211: Machinery remains mounted on the stern deck. Photo by Tamara Thomsen.

Fig. 212 (top): The hatch opening in the stern deck allows a view of the interior. Photo by Tamara Thomsen.
Fig. 213 (bottom): The bend in the side of this huge section of the hull shows the power of nature. Photo by Tamara Thomsen.

Improving Dive Site Access

The Great Lakes Shipwreck Preservation Society (GLSPS) worked with the Minnesota Department of Natural Resources to improve access to the shore entry point for divers wishing to visit the *Madeira*. The GLSPS also provided a more accurate drawing of the shipwreck, which became part of a sign posted near the beach entry. The Department of Natural Resources (DNR) has implemented many of the group's suggestions: divers will find more information at the shore entry point, expanded parking, restroom facilities, and easier access to the beach.

The GLSPS places mooring buoys on the shipwreck each spring and removes them each fall. The group also monitors the condition of the shipwreck and provides this information to the DNR.

Clockwise from bottom left
Fig. 214: Two mooring buoys mark the bow and stern of the *Madeira* at Gold Rock Point.
Fig. 215: An enlarged parking lot with gated entry is reserved for use by divers. The kiosk has helpful information.
Fig. 216: The wider, shorter, and smoother trail provides convenient access to the beach.
Fig. 217: The new wooden steps leading to the beach.
Fig. 218: The Gitchi-Gami State Trail passes in front of the vehicle entry area.
Photos by Stephen B. Daniel.

Historic Artifact in Lake Superior near Beaver Bay

Charlie

The two-masted wooden merchant schooner, originally named *Charley* (changed to *Charlie* in 1867 shipping records), was built by John B. Mayer in 1863 in Bark Shanty Point, Michigan (known today as Saginaw Bay). The ship was single-decked, with a length of 61 feet, a beam of 18 feet, and a draft of 6 feet. The bow was plain and the stern square; the ship grossed 80 to 95 tons.[76] The small schooner started out carrying lumber, fish, and general cargo in the Saginaw Bay and St. Clair River areas.

Fig. 219: The schooner *Charlie* in the Duluth Harbor (date unknown). Courtesy of Minnesota Historical Society / State Historic Preservation Office.

In 1866, it was refitted by a new master in Sandusky, Ohio, increasing the length (perhaps with a new bowsprit) to 62 feet 8.5 inches.

The *Charlie* was sold in 1867 to Albert Wieland of Detroit. Its home port was changed to Beaver Bay, Minnesota, and it carried lumber from Wieland's sawmill in Beaver Bay to Duluth and other ports around Lake Superior. The *Charlie* also carried farm produce for Wieland.[77] It spent winters in the Duluth Harbor, listing its home port as Superior, Wisconsin, in 1871.

Still working along the North Shore in 1874, the schooner ran aground at Madeline Island in July. It was towed to Duluth, with pumps running to keep it afloat, and it was repaired and returned to service.

Two different accounts note the demise of the *Charlie*. On July 10, 1881, a northeaster gale blew the *Charlie* broadside onto the beach while it was attempting to dock at the wharf in Beaver Bay. According to one account, the small schooner resisted the efforts of tugs *Siskiwit* and *Danforth*, which tried to remove it from the beach. The efforts of the tugs proved fruitless, leaving the storm to batter it in its beached position. Another historical accounting states that the schooner was trapped at the wharf during the northeaster, causing the ship to be severely damaged. Efforts were supposedly undertaken to rebuild it, but there is no mention that this was ever accomplished.

Some small chinaware was found near the schooner anchor by Stan Braun in 2002. These artifacts are in excellent shape and suggest that they may be from the *Charlie*. The items have been documented and reported to the Minnesota Historical Society / State Historic Preservation office.

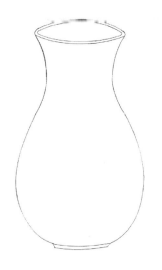

Fig. 220: White china vase or pitcher. Fig. 221: White china cup (without any handle), both found near the anchor and believed to be from the *Charlie*. Drawings by Stephen B. Daniel.

112

Fig. 222: The schooner *Charlie* at the wharf in Beaver Bay. Painting by Mrs. James Lowry, courtesy of Bay Area Historical Society, Duluth, Minnesota.

DIVING THE *CHARLIE* ANCHOR

Type of Artifact	Folding stock anchor
Location	Edge of the reef near the shore, below the town of Beaver Bay
GPS Coordinates	47°15.314′ N, 91°21.591′ W
Depth	78 feet
Dive Rating	Intermediate diver

Since the land above this site is privately owned, this is a boat dive. You can launch from the Silver Bay Marina Boat Ramp north of Beaver Bay off Highway 61. The relatively flat sand-and-rock bottom does not provide much for an anchor to grip. This could be a potential problem in windy weather because of the close proximity of the dive site to shore.

The small schooner anchor is caught in some rocks and rests on its side in 78 feet of water. The anchor, measuring 4 feet by 3.3 feet, is next to the edge of the sloping rocky reef that comes toward the lake from shore. The bottom near the anchor is sand. Some debris from what appears to be a wreck may be located nearby. A partially buried hatch cover suggests this may be the site of the *Charlie* shipwreck.

Divers have made efforts to search the bottom toward deeper water for more clues as to the whereabouts of the *Charlie* shipwreck, but they have been frustrated by the considerable sediment from the taconite tailings that were dumped in the lake for many years by the Reserve Mining Company.

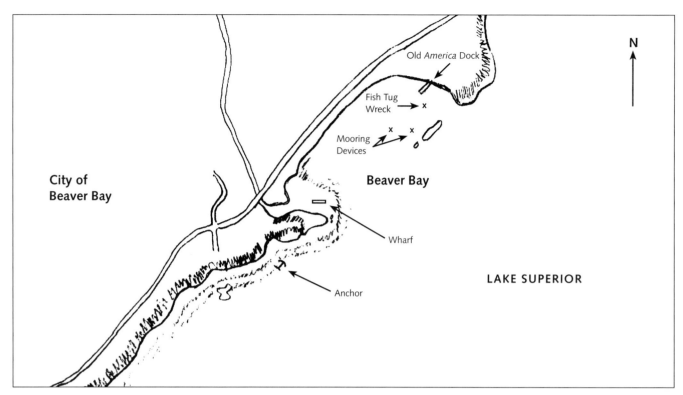

Map 27: The *Charlie* anchor, cribbing from an old wharf (see pp. 115–16), fish tug wreckage, and mooring devices (see pp. 120–21) are all divable sites around Beaver Bay. Drawn by Stephen B. Daniel.

Fig. 223: Anchor believed to be from the schooner *Charlie*. Drawing by Stephen B. Daniel.

Historic Artifacts in Lake Superior at Beaver Bay

PART 1

Wharf

The Wieland family operated a lumber mill in Beaver Bay in the late 1800s. The city constructed a wharf near the mouth of the Beaver River to provide a dock for ship. The schooner *Charlie* (see pp. 112–14) was a frequent visitor, since it was owned by Mr. Wieland and hauled his lumber to Duluth and other ports around the lake head.

The wharf was constructed of cribs made with fourteen- to sixteen-inch-diameter timbers. It was located about 125 feet offshore from the beach southwest of the river mouth. The timbers were fastened with tree nails at fifteen-foot intervals, where the stringers were notched out to hold heavy timbers.[78] Poles that were about six inches in diameter were placed close together between heavy vertical timbers to form the crib. The dock may have been L-shaped, based on a painting showing the *Charlie* tied next to the wharf (see fig. 222). The cribs were filled with rock, most of which has been washed out from the cribs over time. After highways were built, the wharf was no longer used. Storms contributed to its deterioration over time.

DIVING THE BEAVER BAY WHARF

Type of Artifact	Cribbing constructed of timbers
Location	Southwest side of Beaver Bay, about 125 feet offshore from the sand beach southwest of the river mouth and rock bluff
Depth	12 feet
Dive	Novice diver

This is a boat dive (see map 27, p. 114). While this site may seem close to shore, the shore near the site is private property. And there is no easy way to get dive gear to this site from the road. Beware of wind that may blow your boat toward shallow water and the beach. The best time to dive this site is during dry times, such as late summer, when the river is low, because there is less current at the mouth, and the visibility is better.

The cribbing is a timber structure fastened together with large nails. Rocks cover part of the structure on the side facing the bay. The timbers are more visible on the shore side of the structure.

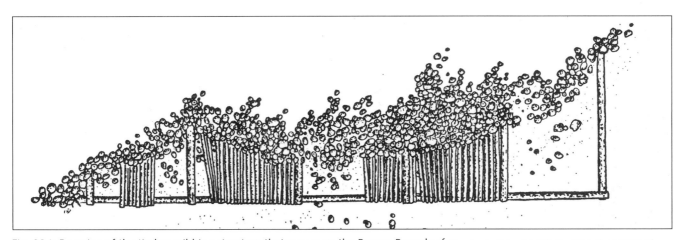

Fig. 224: Remains of the timber cribbing structure that was once the Beaver Bay wharf. Drawing by Tidewater Atlantic Research, courtesy of Minnesota Historical Society / State Historic Preservation Office.

Fig. 225: Site of Beaver Bay wharf, off the point, near the mouth of the Beaver River. Photo by Stephen B. Daniel.

Boat Wreck in Lake Superior at Beaver Bay

Just for Fun

Diving historic shipwrecks is both fascinating and fun. However, as the number of divers visiting a shipwreck underwater increases, there is more wear and tear on fragile parts of the ship. An intentional sinking provides an additional resource for divers to use. The Great Lakes Shipwreck Preservation Society (GLSPS) undertook the *Just for Fun* project to develop a process that would lead to a Sink-a-Ship program at a future date.

The managers of the Knife River Marina contacted the GLSPS in 1998 regarding a thirty-seven-foot ferro-cement sailboat that had been abandoned at the marina for several years. The marina wanted to clear the boatyard of the derelict hull and thought it would be of interest. The GLSPS contacted a number of government agencies and determined what was necessary to conduct an intentional sinking in Lake Superior along the North Shore. The City of Beaver Bay agreed to sponsor the sinking, and several of its council members participated in the event.

Meanwhile, the GLSPS officers and members assumed the task of cleaning the hull and preparing it for sinking. The engine, cabin, and bulwarks had already been removed. Some remaining metal and wood protrusions were taken out to avoid becoming a potential snag on divesuits; the hull was then pressure cleaned to remove residue and any chemicals from fuel or other sources.

A new tiller was fabricated and fastened in place so that the hull could be steered behind a tow boat. All holes were plugged with devices that could be removed to allow water to enter and fill the boat at the appropriate time. The U.S. Coast Guard was contacted to inspect the hull and approve it for the planned intentional sinking.

The *Just for Fun* was towed to Beaver Bay on June 11, 1999. The next day, more than two hundred people, including media representatives, observed the event. The only difficulty encountered was that it took about two hours for the ferro-cement sailboat hull to sink! The

Fig. 226: The abandoned ferro-cement sailboat hull donated to the GLSPS. Photo by Stephen B. Daniel.

Just for Fun eventually settled on the bottom of the bay and became a new dive attraction.

DIVING THE *JUST FOR FUN*

Type of Vessel	Ferro-cement sailboat hull
Location	Northwest side of Beaver Bay, at the mooring buoy, offshore from the culvert
GPS Coordinates	47°15.56' N, 91°17.15' W
Depth	30 feet
Dive Rating	Novice diver

This is a boat dive. Reconstruction of the slope by the road as part of the Gitchi-Gami State Trail prevents shore access for this boat wreck. The GLSPS has placed a mooring buoy to mark the position of the *Just for Fun*. The best launch site is the boat ramp at the Silver Bay Marina, which has a special divers' dock you can use to load your gear.

The thirty-seven-foot ferro-cement sailboat has seen some deterioration over the few years it has been underwater. The port side is starting to cave in, with the chicken wire structure becoming visible as the cement deteriorates. The small wreck is still interesting to dive and serves as an excellent training site for wreck diving.

Other artifacts are located in the general area around the sailboat toward the center of the bay. Make sure to take a divers-down flag with you if you venture out into the bay away from the *Just for Fun*.

Fig. 227: Ken Merryman uses a saws-all tool to cut pieces of the wooden bulkheads from the underside of the deck. All protrusions were removed to make the sailboat hull as safe as possible for diving. Courtesy of Ron Johnson, Golden Valley, Minnesota.

Fig. 228: Tim Tamlyn pries loose metal pieces from the hull to prevent them from becoming a potential snag to a diver's drysuit. Loose fragments of the wooden bulkheads, as well as some fittings, were also removed to provide convenient diver access to the inside of the hull. Courtesy of Ron Johnson, Golden Valley, Minnesota.

Fig. 229 (left): Ken Merryman cleans the outside of the hull with a high-pressure water spray to remove loose paint and any contaminants that might be on the surface. The inside of the ferro-cement hull was also pressure-cleaned to remove residue and potential contaminants to prevent them from entering the lake. Courtesy of Ron Johnson, Golden Valley, Minnesota.

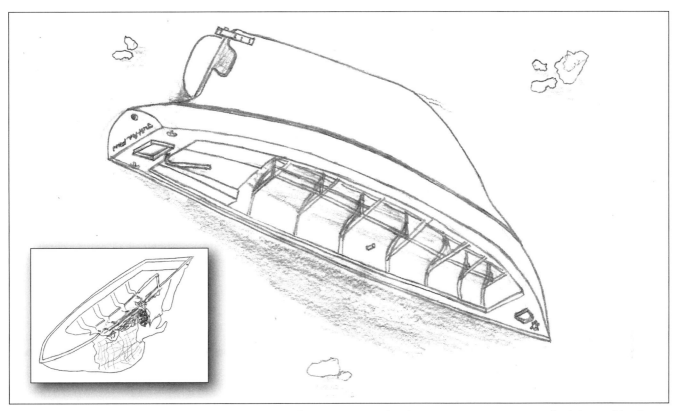

Fig. 230: The *Just for Fun* as it appeared on the bottom after the intentional sinking. Fig. 231 (inset): How it had changed by the summer of 2002. Drawings by Stephen B. Daniel.

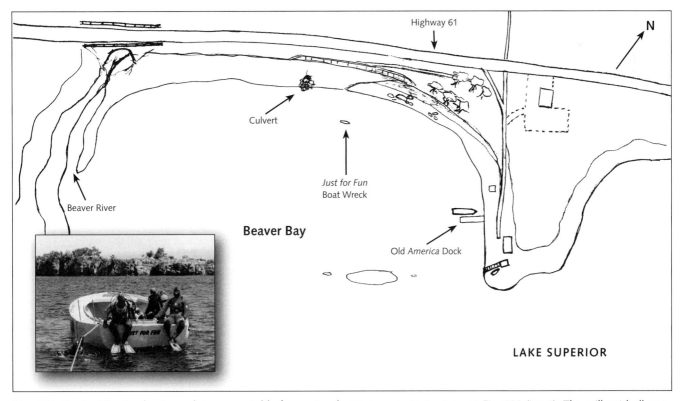

Map 28: The *Just for Fun* boat wreck is very suitable for novice divers. Drawn by Stephen B. Daniel. Fig. 232 (inset): The sailboat hull was positioned over the intended dive site. The divers on board removed the plugs from several openings in the hull to let the water in, and then they waited anxiously in anticipation of the sinking. Courtesy of Ron Johnson, Golden Valley, Minnesota.

Historic Artifacts in Lake Superior at Beaver Bay

PART 2

Fish Tug Wreck and Mooring Debris

Underwater visitors to Beaver Bay have an opportunity to see part of an old fish tug on the bottom. Only part of the bow and some small sections of the hull planking and frames remain. The identity of the small vessel is not known, but it resembles the fish tug *Nor Shor*, which is located on land at the northeast side of the bay. (Note that the tug is on private property, which is posted "no trespassing.") This tug is typical of the type used by commercial fishermen along the North Shore for many years.

Wooden fish tugs similar to the *Nor Shor* were built in the 1940s and used through the 1960s. The forward section of the tug housed a working area where fishermen would haul nets through the openings in the side and remove the catch. A long table might be built in the center of the tug to enable the crew to work in a protected area. Some boats had portholes to allow light into this area, while others used electric lights powered by the engine.

Outside the Bayfield Maritime Museum is a restored example of a fish tug. The pilot in the fish tug would stand in a cabin above the engine at the rear of the tug, steering with the tug's wheel while peering through the narrow windshield. The fish tugs had few portholes to help protect them from heavy seas. The fish tug in Bayfield also had metal sheathing fastened over the wooden hull to help make the boat more durable.

Commercial fishermen moored their fishing boats in Beaver Bay, which afforded protection from stormy weather, especially in the lee of the small island on the northeast side of the bay. The boats may have encountered problems when a northeaster would roll into the bay, however. This was the type of storm that wrecked the schooner *Charlie* on the southeast end of the bay. Perhaps this fish tug succumbed to a fierce northeaster gale sometime in the past, and now some of its bones are on the bottom of the bay. Today almost no fish tugs remain

Fig. 233: The *Nor Shor* on land at the east end of Beaver Bay. Photo by Stephen B. Daniel.

in use on Lake Superior, because there are so few commercial fishermen. But the wreck of one tug remains as a reminder of recent history.

DIVING THE HISTORIC ARTIFACTS IN BEAVER BAY

Type of Artifacts	Section of fish tug wreck, mooring devices, metal tub
Location	Artifacts are scattered across the bottom of the bay
Depth	35 feet
Dive Rating	Novice diver

This is a boat dive. Reconstruction of the slope by the road as part of the Gitchi-Gami State Trail prevents shore access for this area (see map 27, p. 114). It should be noted that the old *America* dock is *not* available for use by divers. The Silver Bay Marina has an excellent boat launch with a special divers' dock you can use to load gear. The marina is a short distance away in the next bay north of Beaver Bay.

Some wreckage from an old fish tug may be seen about seventy-five feet southwest of the old *America* dock. The wreckage consists of the bow stem section of the tug. Some other wreckage nearby may move around when storms pass through the bay.

Several interesting mooring devices may be seen on the bottom. Beaver Bay was used for many years by commercial fishermen, who moored their fish tugs to these devices on the bottom. Often things would be dropped overboard or discarded when they were no longer needed. Divers may find a variety of items on the bottom, including a tire, a rusty axe, and a shovel. Pieces of broken china may also be seen in some areas of the bay. Any artifacts you find should remain in place to be preserved underwater for future divers to view them.

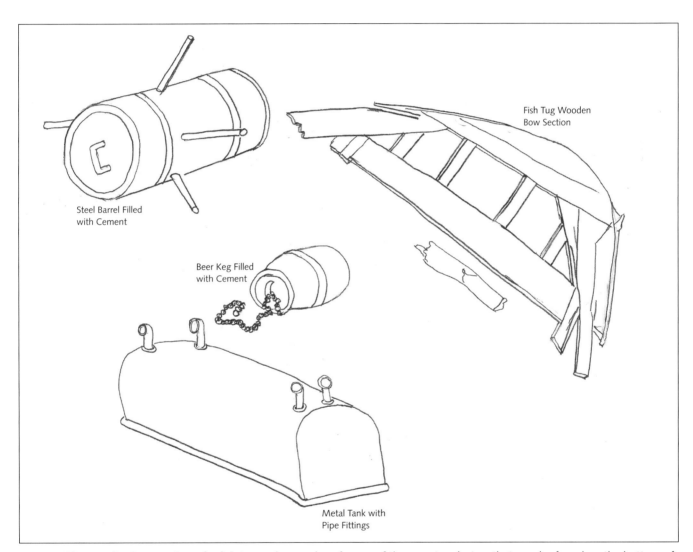

Fig. 234: The wooden bow section of a fish tug and examples of some of the mooring devices that may be found on the bottom of Beaver Bay. Drawing by Stephen B. Daniel.

Shipwrecks in Lake Superior at Silver Bay

Hesper

The *Hesper*, a wooden bulk freight steamer, was built by the Ship Owners' Drydock Company at the Radcliff yard and launched in Cleveland, Ohio, on June 27, 1890. It was 250 feet long and grossed 2,700 tons;[79] its beam was 41 feet, and its depth of hold was 20 feet. The ship had two decks, three masts, a plain head, and a rounded stern. Its owners, the Bradley Transportation Company, named the ship after the evening star (also Atlas's brother in Greek mythology).

The *Hesper*'s single propeller was powered by a vertical triple-expansion steam engine built by the Cleveland Shipbuilding Company. The engine produced 825 horsepower with two Scotch boilers, which vented through a single smokestack. The 12-foot-diameter propeller was attached in sections with a 14-foot pitch.

The ship originally carried two folding stock anchors. In 1899, the center mast and one deck were removed, leaving it with two spar poles and a single deck. The *Hesper* was involved in the wrecking of the *Samuel P. Ely* (see pages 65–67) on October 31, 1896. It survived that gale only to sink in a storm in 1905.

The Sinking

The *Hesper* was running light and heading for Silver Bay to pick up a load of ore when a spring snowstorm on May 4, 1905, caused it to drift off course. The ship was thrown against the reef on the southwest side of Silver Bay Harbor by the sixty-mile-an-hour northeaster gale. As the stack fell, the cabins and spars were washed overboard. The captain and crew stayed on board until it was certain the ship would not survive the heavy storm. Then they launched the lifeboats and made it safely to shore.

The deck of the ship tore away when a huge wave lifted the hull off the reef and slid it into forty feet of water. The storm continued to break up the ship, sending

Fig. 235: The *Hesper* passing through the Sault Ste. Marie Locks around 1895. Courtesy of Historical Collections of the Great Lakes, Bowling Green State University, Ohio.

parts adrift along the shore for about five miles.[80] The captain and crew were given shelter in Beaver Bay, where they informed the owners of the loss. J. B. Wanless and his tug *Sara Smith* salvaged the ship's engines, boilers, propeller, and shaft.[81] He may also have removed one of the anchors, since it does not appear near the shipwreck. Some Great Lakes Shipwreck Preservation Society (GLSPS) members who are also members of the

Fig. 236: The *Hesper* entering the Milwaukee River around 1900. Courtesy of Great Lakes Marine Collection, Milwaukee Public Library / Wisconsin Marine Historical Society.

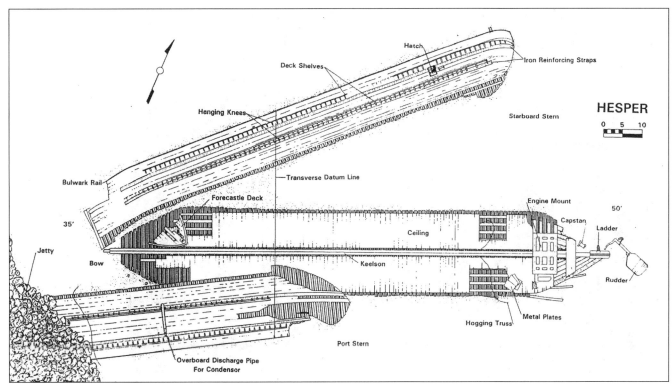

Fig. 237: The *Hesper* shipwreck. The bow of the port side of the hull is buried under the breakwater. A mooring buoy, maintained by the GLSPS, is fastened to the stern section of the bottom of the ship. Courtesy of Minnesota Historical Society / State Historic Preservation Office.

Owatonna Dive Club are trying to clear gravel away from what they think is the shank of the port bow anchor. Minnesota's State Historic Preservation Office gave the GLSPS permission to expose the anchor underwater, so that others may enjoy viewing it.

The Shipwreck

The *Hesper* shipwreck extends out from the eastern side of the west breakwater in Silver Bay. Following the sinking, the ship was blown apart to avoid it becoming a hazard to navigation. Divers will find the bottom section in the center of three main sections of the wreck. The bow of the ship faces toward the breakwater. The starboard side rests on the sandy bottom adjacent to the starboard bow of the bottom section and extends out into the bay. The port section is half buried under the breakwater.

Divers will see many knees, which once supported the main deck, along each side of the ship. The main deck and cabins are gone, probably from storms over the years. Only a piece of the forecastle remains, lying on the starboard side of the keel at the bow. A discharge pipe is still attached to the port side of the ship near the rear section. A hatch opening in the starboard side of the ship can be seen toward the rear.

The heavy-timbered keelson is visible along the entire bottom of the ship. Huge bolts protrude from the engine mount at the stern. Some metal plates are visible on the port side of the stern. Look for the stern capstan partially buried in sand and gravel on the starboard side of the stern. A ladder is located nearby. One of the most interesting artifacts on the shipwreck is the large rudder, with the rudder post intact, next to the pointed stern. Look

Fig. 238: Bronze capstan head, displayed in the Lake Superior Maritime Visitor Center in Duluth, Minnesota. Courtesy of Minnesota Historical Society / State Historic Preservation Office.

closely to find the draft marks painted on the rudder.

A broken propeller fluke is located next to the rudder. This large artifact was returned to the shipwreck through the GLSPS Put-It-Back program in 1998. The fluke broke off the ship's prop at the reef by Pellet Island.

DIVING THE *HESPER*

Type of Vessel	Wooden bulk freight steamer
Location	Northeast side of west breakwater, Silver Bay
GPS Coordinates	47°16.25′ N, 91°16.30′ W
Depth	40–60 feet
Dive Rating	Novice diver

Look for the diver path that leads from the roadside drop-off point on the breakwater down a series of steps to the water. Use caution when entering and exiting the water when waves are present. The shipwreck starts at the breakwater to the right.

This is also a boat dive. You may launch your boat from one of the ramps or the divers' dock at the Silver Bay Marina. Remember to use proper boat ramp etiquette and stage your boat in the parking lot up the hill, not at the ramp. The *Hesper* shipwreck is marked with a mooring buoy. The site is listed on the National Register of Historic Places, so it is protected.

Fig. 239: A diver prepares to enter the water near the *Hesper*. Courtesy of Ken Merryman, Fridley, Minnesota.

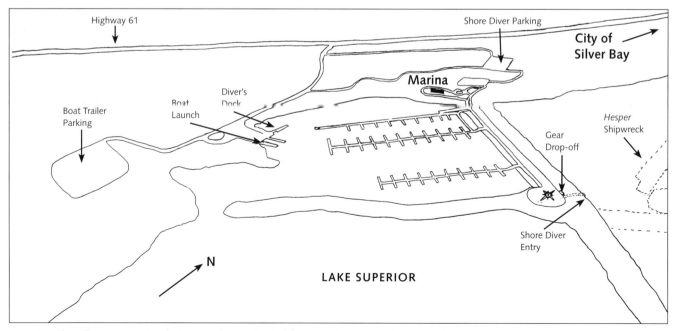

Map 29: The Silver Bay Marina has many diver-oriented features. Drawn by Stephen B. Daniel.

Fig. 240 (top): The bilge pump was returned to the *Hesper* shipwreck as a GLSPS project. Photo by Tamara Thomsen.
Fig. 241 (bottom): The forecastle deck at the bow of the ship is still intact. Photo by Tamara Thomsen.

Fig. 242 (top): The capstan is revealed in the gravel bottom near the stern. Photo by Tamara Thomsen.
Fig. 243 (bottom): Rods protruding from bottom beams show where the engine was mounted. Photo by Tamara Thomsen.

Fig. 244 (top): A porthole opening is visible under the main deck shelf. Photo by Tamara Thomsen.
Fig. 245 (bottom): A workbench is fastened to the hull near the hatch on the starboard side. Photo by Tamara Thomsen.

Fig. 246 (top): The steering quadrant and emergency tiller are attached to the top of the rudder post. Photo by Tamara Thomsen.
Fig. 247 (bottom): The upper (main) and lower deck support shelves are attached to the inside of the hull. Photo by Tamara Thomsen.

The Silver Bay Marina

The Minnesota Department of Natural Resources (DNR) began construction of a new marina at Silver Bay in 1998 as part of the Safe Harbor program. The marina was completed in 2000 and includes a marine office for the harbor master. The new slips make it convenient for boaters to enjoy the lake, and the boat launch was expanded to four boat ramps. A divers' dock was added to the north side of the boat launch to make loading boats more efficient. The parking lot was expanded up the hill to accommodate more vehicles and boat trailers.

The facilities are excellent, with ample parking, electricity, water, and restrooms with showers. A comfortable lobby, snack machines, and a fish cleaning station next to the marina building are additional amenities. The park and picnic area near the entrance to the marina were improved as well.

The GLSPS worked with the DNR during the process to improve diver access by boat and by shore. Many improvements were made to make diving safer and more convenient. Divers and boaters alike will be able to use the marina and enjoy pursuing their interests in or on the water for years to come.

Clockwise from left
Fig. 248: A view of the bay from the marina.
Fig. 249: A mooring buoy (note arrow) marks the stern of the *Hesper* and helps keep boats away from shore divers.
Fig. 250: The Silver Bay Marina. Shore divers may drop off their gear on the east side of the flagpole circle. A sign by the rocks marks the path leading down to the water's edge. Courtesy of Minnesota Department of Natural Resources, Trails and Waterways Division.
Fig. 251: The boat launch is located to the west of the marina building. Four ramps accommodate boaters.
Fig. 252: The divers' dock is to be used for loading gear and people into boats.
Photos by Stephen B. Daniel, unless otherwise noted.

Frontenac

The *Frontenac* was built by Great Lakes Engineering Works (GLEW) as hull #244 and launched at River Rouge, Michigan, in 1923. The 604-foot steel bulk freighter built for Cleveland Cliffs grossed 8,158 tons.[82] The first engine was a triple-expansion steam engine built by GLEW. A steam turbine engine built by DeLaval Steam Turbine Company in Trenton, New Jersey, was installed in 1954. The *Frontenac* was one of several lakers that participated in the search for the *Edmund Fitzgerald* following its sinking in a fierce gale on November 10, 1975.

On the night of November 22, 1979, the *Frontenac* was heading up from Duluth to Silver Bay to load a cargo of iron ore at Reserve Mining Company. The captain radioed ahead to the *Armco* to inquire about the harbor weather conditions. The rolling six- to twelve-foot seas

caused by the twenty-five- to thirty-mile-per-hour northeast wind did not seem to be a problem to the captain of the *Frontenac*. The ship passed Silver Bay and turned around to starboard to approach the harbor. As it approached, the green navigation buoy light was visible. A sudden storm squall hit, preventing the ship's master and wheelsman from seeing Pellet Island. To make matters worse, the privately maintained light on the island was not lit that night.[83]

The ship hit the reef and stuck on the rocks as the waves rocked it closer to the island. The continued action of the wind and waves caused considerable damage to the vessel. The Coast Guard cutter *Mesquite* came out from Duluth to assist the ship. After fuel oil was pumped out by the fuel lighter *Reiss Marine*, the ship was able to float off the reef enough that it could be towed over to the Reserve Mining dock. Workers from Fraser Shipyards

Fig. 253: The *Frontenac* passing under the Blatnik Bridge, with Duluth in the background. Photo by Al Sweigert, courtesy of Lake Superior Maritime Collection, University of Wisconsin–Superior.

welded plates to the hull inside to reinforce the bottom. The Coast Guard then determined the ship was able to return to Duluth for additional examination and repairs. The *Frontenac* left for Duluth on November 28 and was put in dry dock at Fraser Shipyards in Superior, Wisconsin. Damage was found to be much more extensive (over three hundred feet of the hull had been damaged), with a section of the keel being pushed up inside the empty ship during the grounding.[84] Crews welded new steel plates

to most of the bottom before the ship was moved to a winter berth near Superior. For the next ten days the ship listed to port. It was finally scrapped in Superior in 1985, after it was determined to be no longer seaworthy. The pilothouse was donated to the Two Harbors Lighthouse Museum, where it can be seen today.

Since Cleveland Cliffs sold the *Frontenac* to Fraser Shipyards for scrapping, there is nothing left for divers to see on the reef in Silver Bay.

Fig. 254 (above): View of the port side of the *Frontenac*, hard against the rocks. Photo by Carl Curtis, *Duluth News Tribune*, courtesy of Lake Superior Maritime Collection, University of Wisconsin–Superior.

Fig. 255 (left): The *Frontenac* almost touches the southwest breakwater. Photo by the Minnesota Air National Guard.

Fig. 256 (above): Pilothouse of the *Frontenac* at Two Harbors Lighthouse Museum, Two Harbors, Minnesota. Photo by Stephen B. Daniel.

Fig. 257 (left): Inspecting hull damage after the storm. Courtesy of Lake Superior Maritime Collection, University of Wisconsin–Superior.

Fig. 258 (below): Interior view of the pilothouse showing the navigation equipment and helm. Photo by Stephen B. Daniel.

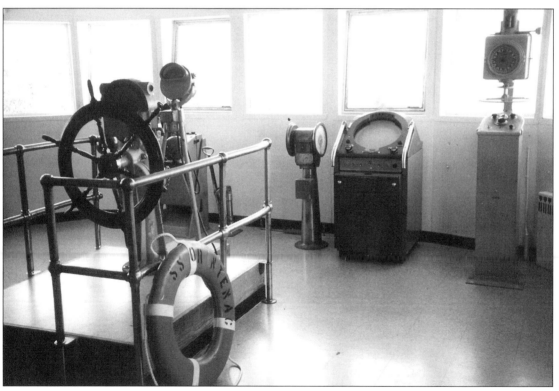

Underwater Geology

PART 4

Sea Caves, Palisade Head

The massive geologic structure of Palisade Head provides an impressive view of Lake Superior high above the water. This rocky precipice is located north of Silver Bay, off of Highway 61. A small road winds up to a parking lot at the top of the cliff, where visitors may walk to an overlook.

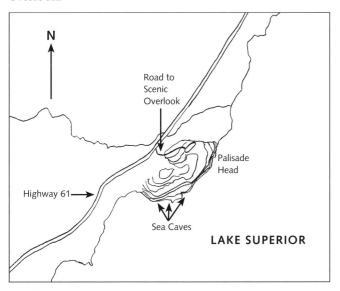

DIVING PALISADE HEAD

Type of Structure	Sea caves
Location	North of Silver Bay
Depth	10 feet
Dive Rating	Novice diver

The sea caves are located at the base of the cliff structure. They may be reached only by boat because of the sheer cliff structure above. It is best to consider diving this site when seas are calm: the rocky bottom can make securing an anchor difficult when wind and waves are present. As you swim in and out of the small sea caves, you can observe the fascinating underwater rock structures up close.

Map 30: Palisade Head has a scenic overlook and parking area. Drawn by Stephen B. Daniel.

Fig. 259: Sea caves at the base of Palisade Head, north of Silver Bay. Photo by Stephen B. Daniel.

Historic Artifacts in Lake Superior at Crystal Bay

3M Dock Cribs

In 1902, the Minnesota Mining and Manufacturing Company (3M), with offices located in the Dwan Building in Two Harbors, operated a mine to obtain corundum, a very hard mineral made of aluminum oxide mixed with crystals of varying colors. The company intended to sell the mineral to grinding wheel manufacturers on the east coast. The mine was located up the hill at Illgen City, where Highway 1 intersects Highway 61. The mined rock was processed in a building next to the mine and then transported down the hill to a dock that extended out from shore in Crystal Bay. Ships would load the processed ore at the dock and carry it in bulk to Duluth.

When this ore proved to be ineffective as an abrasive material, the mining was discontinued.

The dock at Crystal Bay was supported by cribbing. A cement structure on shore facilitated the loading of the refined ore onto ships. The cribbing remains on the sandy bottom today. The light-colored shapes of the crib may be observed from the small cliff on the shore above, to the southwest. The foundation of the cement structure, although overgrown by foliage, is still visible on shore next to a culvert that runs underneath the road.

Divers or snorkelers may visit the underwater crib structure by entering the water either from shore or from a boat.

Fig. 260: The original building next to the 3M mine was used to process ore as it was removed from the ground. Courtesy of 3M.

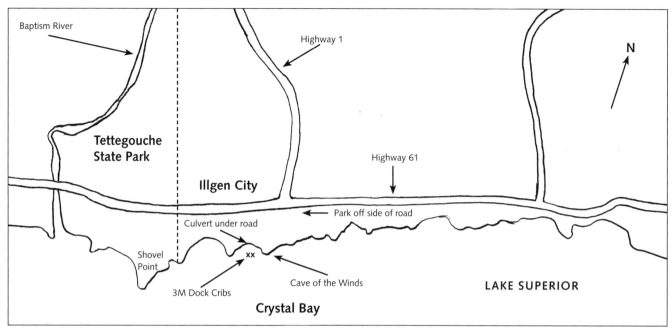

Map 31: The 3M dock cribs and the Cave of the Winds (see p. 137) are both located near Illgen City. Drawn by Stephen B. Daniel.

DIVING THE DOCK CRIBS

Type of Structure	Wooden crib
Location	Next to the beach at Illgen City in Crystal Bay
Depth	10–21 feet
Dive Rating	Novice Diver

This dive site may be accessed from shore by parking off the shoulder of Highway 61, northeast of the guardrail. You will need to carry your gear down the hillside to the beach. This is a steep drop, requiring caution. Once at the beach, you may gear up and enter the water at the beach in front of the cement structure that is located in the foliage next to the large culvert under the road.

This dive site may also be reached by boat. Two anchors are recommended, since you will need to come close to shore and the sea cave to the northeast. Check the security of the anchors; you may need to pile some rocks on them to hold them in place.

You will find the crib structure about fifteen feet offshore, at about a ten-foot depth. The cribbing extends into the lake approximately seventy-five feet. The structure is taller in deeper water. A second, shorter crib structure is located to the southwest, just off the beach about forty feet from the large crib structure.

The Cave of the Winds is nearby and an easy swim from the cribbing structure; see page 137 for more information.

Fig. 261: Remains of cribbing used to support the docks are located at the base of the hill, out from the beach. Photo by Stephen B. Daniel.

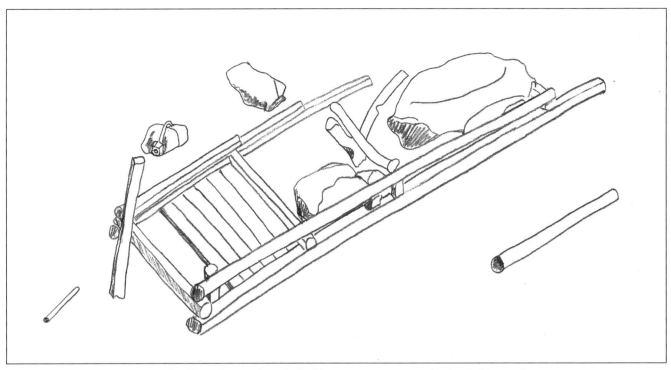

Fig. 262: The crib structure is built of large logs with a planked bottom to support rocks that held it in place. Drawing by Stephen B. Daniel.

Underwater Geology

PART 5

Cave of the Winds, Crystal Bay

The Cave of the Winds is a natural opening in the rocky cliff on the northeastern side of Crystal Bay. The cave may be observed on the surface from a small boat. Divers may enjoy the greatest experience, as they may see the geological formation from both above and below the surface of the water.

DIVING THE CAVE OF THE WINDS

Type of Structure	Sea cave
Location	Crystal Bay, near Illgen City
Depth	10–12 feet inside the cave
Dive Rating	Novice diver

The cave is in the shape of an L and may be entered through a rectangular opening at either end. Swimming into the opening on the eastern, or lake side, may be best because it enables you to end up in sheltered water by the shore near the south side.

Boulders and interesting shapes on the rocky bottom may be observed underwater. Some surge may be experienced while swimming through the cave because of the force of the wave action moving water through the cave. Swim through for an interesting tour of the cave bottom, and while you're inside, stop midway and surface to observe the rock structure above the water line.

Fig. 263: The Cave of the Winds is located on the northeastern edge of Crystal Bay. Photo by Stephen B. Daniel.

Shipwrecks in Lake Superior at Thomasville

George Spencer

The wooden bulk freight steamer *George Spencer* was built by Thomas Quayle & Sons in 1884 and launched at Cleveland, Ohio.[85] The vessel was built for Thomas Wilson to haul coal and iron ore. The ship was 230.5 feet long with a beam of 37.2 feet. Its hold was 18.8 feet deep, and it grossed 1,360 tons.

THE SINKING

Different stories relate the fate of the *George Spencer*. One story claims that it was refloated to sail again, but no mention of the *Spencer* after the date of the sinking has been found in historical records. Another version says it was too damaged in the grounding and left to the elements. The wreck structure in the water is different from that on shore, suggesting that it is from a second ship.

The *Spencer* was towing the schooner *Amboy* toward Duluth when the ships were overcome by the *Mataafa* Storm on November 28, 1905. Both ships got lost and went aground at Thomasville. The *Amboy* was blown broadside onto the beach, while the *Spencer* lodged on the rocky bottom in shallow water, facing shore.

The sailors from both ships were rescued by local fishermen, who waded out into the surf to grab lines

Fig. 264: The *George Spencer*. Courtesy of C. Patrick Labadie Collection, Lake Superior Maritime Collection, University of Wisconsin–Superior.

tossed by the crew. The lines were fastened to trees so that the officers and crew could use a breeches buoy to get everyone ashore. As a result, the entire crews of both ships made it safely to shore, where they received shelter from the settlers nearby. The storm continued to batter the ships through the night.

Newspapers at that time reported that the following day, when the ships were examined, the *Amboy*, which was sideways on the beach, was found to be a total wreck, with its back broken.[86] The *Spencer*, on the other hand, appeared to look alright, with its hatches intact.[87] Outward appearances seemed to suggest that it might be refloated and resume its shipping career. However, the ships were traveling light, without cargo, when they were upbound for Duluth and may have proved difficult to remove. It may also have been determined at a later time that the grounding had damaged the bottom of the ship beyond repair.

Today the remains of a hull bottom typical of a wooden steamer rest in shallow water facing toward shore: this suggests that the *Spencer* was never refloated. The remains of the keelson of a separate large ship, broadside on the stony beach, may be what is left of the schooner *Amboy*.

A section of the side of a ship is located in water near the beach to the northeast of the *Spencer* wreckage, but it

is difficult to determine which ship it may be from. Time, weather, and possible scavenging over the years have caused the deterioration of much of the wreckage.

The configuration of the bottom of the hull is representative of the type of hull structure of the steamer *Spencer*. There are additional pieces of hull nearby. It is likely that the ship was determined to be unseaworthy and its machinery salvaged for use in another vessel. The hull was probably abandoned to the elements and deteriorated over time. This is the largest piece of wreckage in the area. While several pieces of metal lie in deeper water (seventeen to twenty feet), farther into the lake, there do not appear to be any artifacts from the shipwreck nearby.

The *Spencer* and the *Amboy* are listed on the National Register of Historic Places and are therefore protected.

DIVING THE *GEORGE SPENCER* SHIPWRECK

Type of Vessel	Wooden bulk freighter
Location	About 30 feet offshore from the pebble beach at Thomasville
GPS Coordinates	47°28.674' N, 90°59.898' W
Depth	7–12 feet
Dive Rating	Novice diver

Although close to shore, this wreck is best reached by boat, since the beach is private property. The closest boat launch is at Taconite Harbor, about four and a half miles north of the wreck site. You can anchor your boat

Fig. 265: The *George Spencer* in drydock. Courtesy of Jack Messmer, Lancaster, New York.

Fig. 266: The bottom of the shipwreck is located straight out from the bush at the edge of the beach to the right of the house on shore (see arrow). Photo by Stephen B. Daniel.

in about seventeen feet of water and swim in about a hundred yards toward shore. It is recommended that a compass bearing on the bush be taken before swimming toward shore, as visibility may be affected by recent rain or wave action. You may see some metal debris on the bottom along the way. This dive is an easy swim, allowing views of the large hull timbers that make up the bottom structure of the ship.

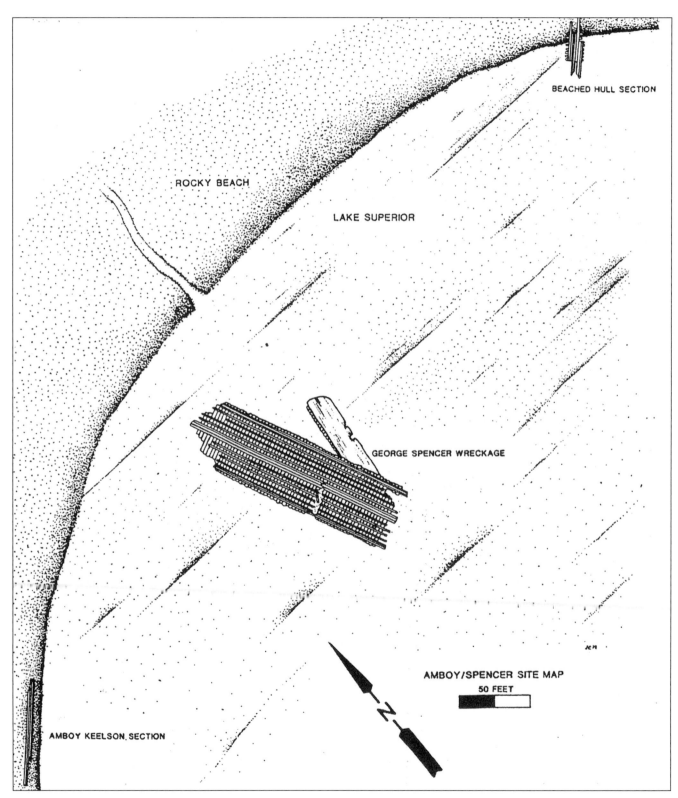

Fig. 267: Site map of the *George Spencer* shipwreck. Drawing by Panamerican Consultants, courtesy of Minnesota Historical Society / State Historic Preservation Office.

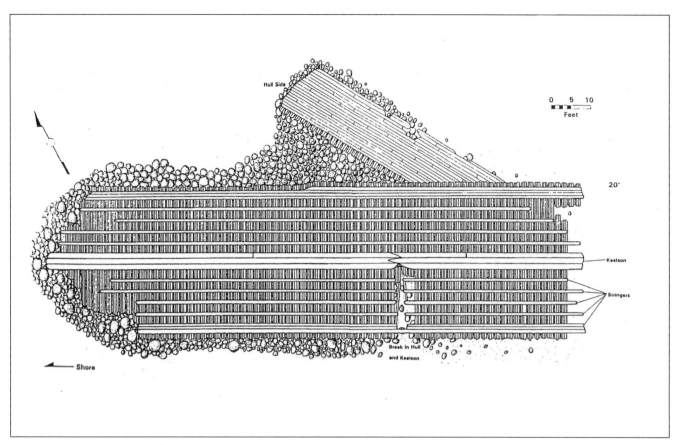

Fig. 268: Bottom of the hull of the *George Spencer*, with a side piece underneath. Drawing by Panamerican Consultants, courtesy of Minnesota Historical Society / State Historic Preservation Office.

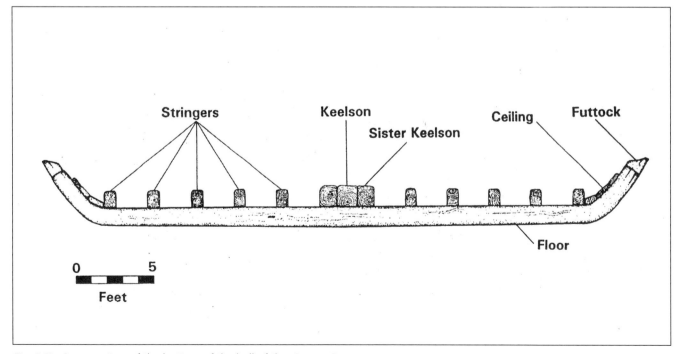

Fig. 269: Cross section of the bottom of the hull of the *George Spencer*. Drawing by Panamerican Consultants, courtesy of Minnesota Historical Society / State Historic Preservation Office.

Fig. 270:
Futtock ends at the side of the *Spencer's* bottom. Photo by Ken Merryman, Fridley, Minnesota.

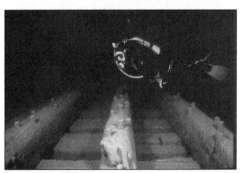

Fig. 271:
A diver swims over the bilge keelsons. Photo by Ken Merryman, Fridley, Minnesota.

Fig. 272:
A diver examines the keelson. Photo by Ken Merryman, Fridley, Minnesota.

Fig. 273:
Keelsons next to the center keelson of the hull bottom. Photo by Ken Merryman, Fridley, Minnesota.

Fig. 274:
A shallow-water view of the ship's hull. Steel pins protrude from the planking and frames. Photo by Elmer Engman, Proctor, Minnesota.

Amboy

The *Amboy* started life on the lakes as the *Helena*, which was built as a three-masted schooner with an oak hull for the Cleveland Transportation Company in 1874.[88] It was 209 feet long, with a beam of 34.2 feet and a hold of 14.4 feet, and grossed 893 tons. The *Helena* carried a figurehead at the bow and had a square stern. The keelson was built with two main timbers and two timbers adjacent as sister keelsons. Both were two timbers high. The schooner had a single deck and a centerboard typical of Great Lakes schooners. After a series of mishaps, the *Helena* was involved in a collision with the steel steamer *Mariska* in July 1891. The *Helena* sank in 30 feet of water with a full load of coal. The insurance company declared it a total loss, selling it to the Milwaukee Tug Boat Company in 1892. The ship was raised and renamed the *Amboy*, serving as a towbarge until it was sold to the Tonawanda Iron & Steel Company of North Tonawanda, New York, in 1899.[89] Thereafter it was put in tow of the wooden steamer *George Spencer*.

THE SINKING

The *Amboy* was being towed empty by the *George Spencer* when they encountered the great *Mataafa* Storm on November 28, 1905. When the *George Spencer* lost its bearings in the snowstorm, the *Amboy* suffered the same fate as its tow steamer, ending up on the beach near Thomasville. (See p. 139 for more about the event.)

The schooner broke its back when huge waves pitched it up broadside on the beach. The ship was declared a total loss and was abandoned on shore. Years of deterioration followed, from the ravages of weather and visitors who removed the oak for firewood or other purposes. The keelson is all that remains on the stony beach today. Steel rods that once held the planking and other structural timbers may be seen protruding from the keelson. Both the *Amboy* and *George Spencer* are protected, since they are listed on the National Register of Historic Places.

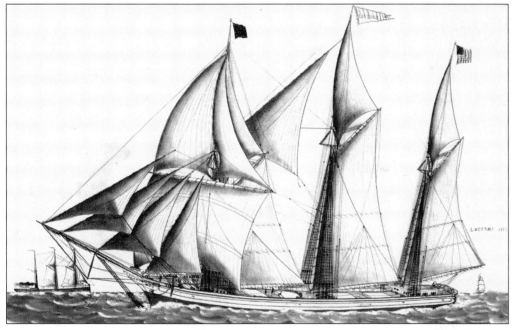

Fig. 275 (above): The
schooner *Verona* and the
steamer *Vienna*. The
Verona was a sister ship
to the *Amboy*. Courtesy of
C. Patrick Labadie Collection, Lake
Superior Maritime Collection,
University of Wisconsin–Superior.

Fig. 276 (left): The *Lu-
cerne*, a schooner of the
same class as the *Amboy*.
Courtesy of the Herman G. Runge
Collection, Milwaukee Public
Library.

Fig. 277 (far left): The
keelson of the hull of
the *Amboy*. Photo by Scott
Anfinson, courtesy of Minnesota
Historical Society / State Historic
Preservation Office.

Fig. 278 (left): The bottom
portion of the hull of the
Amboy. Courtesy of Elmer Engman, Proctor, Minnesota.

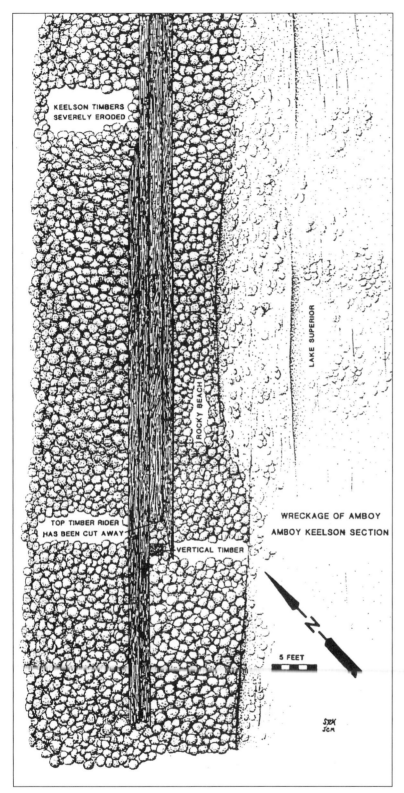

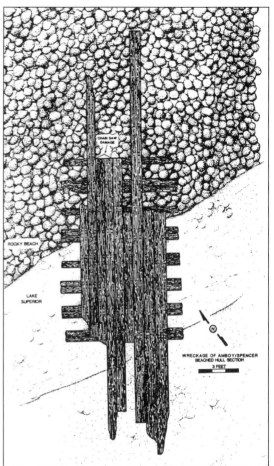

Fig. 279 (above): A section of the hull, most likely from the *Spencer*, rests in the water and extends onto the beach. Drawing by Panamerican Consultants, courtesy of Minnesota Historical Society / State Historic Preservation Office.

Fig. 280 (left): A seventy-four-foot section of the keelson is firmly embedded in the rocks. The construction and location, broadside on the beach, confirm that the wreckage is from the schooner *Amboy*. Drawing by Panamerican Consultants, courtesy of Minnesota Historical Society / State Historic Preservation Office.

Historic Artifacts in Lake Superior at Sugarloaf Cove

Logging Camp

Sugarloaf Cove was the site of logging operations by the Consolidated Paper Company from 1942 until 1971. Pulpwood was cut from the forests in the area during fall and winter, hauled to a place above the cove, and stacked in piles. In the spring the logs would be lifted by crane onto trucks, which would transport them to a chute that hurled them into the water at the cove. Booms held the logs inside the cove until enough were ready to be assembled into a large raft. Thousands of logs were prepared this way each season.

A tug would tow the teardrop-shaped raft of logs along the North Shore and then across the lake to Ashland, Wisconsin. The logs were then processed into paper at local mills.

Diving Sugarloaf Cove

Type of Artifacts	Metal logging implements and chain
Location	22.75 miles north of Silver Bay, 3.3 miles south of Taconite Harbor
Depth	4–16 feet
Dive Rating	Novice diver

Divers may access this site either from shore or by boat. The Sugarloaf Interpretive Center has limited parking by the building. Check with the manager before parking and diving. You can carry your gear down the trail to the stony beach, where you will have an easy entry into the water. For a boat dive, you can launch a boat from the Taconite Harbor Boat Launch, northeast of the interpretive center.

Fig. 281: Aerial photo of the logging operation at Sugarloaf Cove, c. 1957. Courtesy of Northeast Minnesota Historical Center.

The cove is very open and susceptible to wind and waves from the northeast. This situation would often make it difficult for tugs to leave with log rafts when inclement weather was encountered.

The metal artifacts are scattered across the bottom from shallow water out into the center of the cove. You can find the location of the artifacts in the drawing of the cove on display in the Interpretive Center building. A large rusty chain that was once used to secure a log boom across the opening of the cove now lies in a pile just inside the point. Look for the large iron ring fastened to a rock on shore; the chain for the boom used to be connected to this ring. The bottom of the cove includes basalt formations, the result of ancient volcanic activity.

Fig. 282: Artifacts from the logging era on display at the Sugarloaf Cove Interpretive Center. Photo by Stephen B. Daniel.

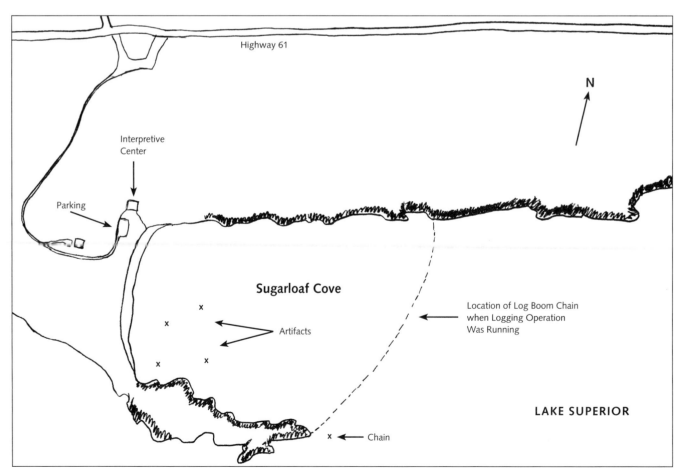

Map 32: The Sugarloaf Cove site features several metal logging artifacts, including a chain. Drawn by Stephen B. Daniel.

GLSPS Helps Survey Sugarloaf Cove

Andrew Slade, director of the Sugarloaf Cove Interpretive Center, wanted to find out if there were more artifacts from the logging operations that used to take place in the cove. He asked Randy Beebe, a Great Lakes Shipwreck Preservation Society (GLSPS) member, for help in conducting an underwater survey of the bottom of the cove. On June 5, 2004, Randy assembled a group of GLSPS volunteers for the project. After listening to a brief history of the cove, the divers were divided into groups to survey different sections of the bottom for logging artifacts. The results were recorded on a drawing of the cove, which included descriptions of the artifacts and their location on the bottom. The survey will enhance the historical information on logging. The Sugarloaf Cove Interpretive Center is located adjacent to Highway 61 and is open to the public.

Fig. 283: **Logging artifact.** Courtesy of Randy Beebe, Duluth, Minnesota.

Fig. 284: **Logging chain.** Photo by Stephen B. Daniel.

Shipwreck in Lake Superior near Taconite Harbor

George Herbert

The *George Herbert* was built for L. R. Martin as a 362-ton freight scow, with 305 net tonnage, and launched at Duluth in 1902.[90] The fifty-five-foot tug *F. W. Gillette* was towing the *Herbert* from Duluth to Two Islands (today known as Taconite Harbor) on the afternoon of November 28, 1905. The ship was carrying supplies to the lumber camps near Two Islands.[91]

The *Herbert* and the *Gillette* encountered a fierce storm that was progressing up the North Shore. The ships took shelter in the lee of the two islands, dropping anchor to wait out the storm. Although the small islands did not offer much protection, they were the only place of refuge for miles in either direction. They hugged the islands for ten hours while the winds howled into the night. Onboard the *Herbert*, the captain and crew of four took turns checking the towline every five minutes. With two men on watch, one would hold his hand on the towline to confirm it was taut while keeping his back to the strong winds, as it was too difficult to see. The other crewman would try to stay warm while waiting his turn to monitor the towline.[92]

At about one A.M., the towline holding the scow snapped, and the *Herbert* was thrust onto the rocky shoreline within minutes. The skipper of the *Herbert*, Captain Charles Johnson, and William Hicks, a clerk at the lumber camp, jumped from the ship and climbed up the rocks to a safer point higher up on shore. The ship began to break up on the rocks below them. The three crewmen—Ole Miller, Ole Nelson, and George Olson—chose not to jump and remained on board; they were killed when the ship was demolished by the wind and waves.

The two survivors spent the night in a settler's cabin nearby. At sunrise the day after the storm, they looked for their fellow seamen but did not see any signs of life among the wreckage on the shore. They found one of the anchors and the broken towline from the scow in the woods about two hundred feet from the lake. They traveled south along the shore to Thomasville, finding the *Spencer* and *Amboy*, which were wrecked in the same storm. They caught a ride on the tug *Crosby* back to Duluth, where they shared their story.

All that remains of the shipwreck today are some remnants of its cargo, debris spread on the bottom of the

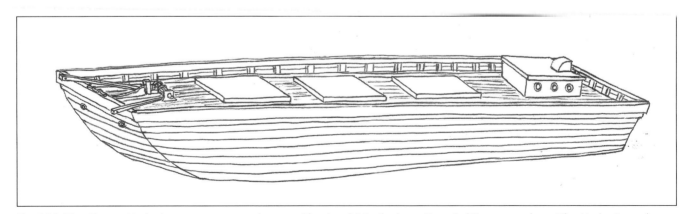

Fig. 285: The *George Herbert* was an unpowered scow with a tow bit in the bow. It carried its own anchors. The *Herbert* may have looked similar to this artist's rendition. Drawing by Stephen B. Daniel.

lake. Nothing remains of the scow itself; the splintered wreckage may have washed away or been used for firewood by residents over the years. The two islands were eventually connected by a rock breakwater to provide protection to freighters docking at the taconite plant. These changes, and the focus on processing iron ore, resulted in a new name for this location: Taconite Harbor. Today, a Safe Harbor has been built by the Minnesota Department of Natural Resources at the southwest end of the harbor to offer shelter from stormy seas.

The wreck site of the *George Herbert* was discovered by Elmer Engman, a shipwreck diving enthusiast and maritime historian from Proctor, Minnesota. He found that the wreck site was marked by a debris field consisting primarily of some cargo.

Remember that all historic artifacts underwater in Lake Superior bordering the North Shore belong to the State of Minnesota. It is illegal to remove any of these items. Please use good diver ethics when you visit this wreck site: take only pictures, and leave only bubbles.

DIVING THE *GEORGE HERBERT*

Type of Artifacts	Logging tools, metal implements, and cable
Location	About 1,000 feet south of the Taconite Harbor Boat Ramp, 50 feet from shore
Depth	40 feet
Dive Rating	Novice diver

This site is accessible only by boat, because the shore terrain is rocky and quite steep. Boats may be launched at the Taconite Harbor Boat Ramp, which is just north of the wreck site. It is a short ride south along the shoreline to the debris field. No marking designates the location of the debris field. The bottom is very rocky. Since this dive site is very close to shore, make sure to check that your anchor is secure before beginning your dive. The debris site is open and may be susceptible to wind and waves from the southeast. Use caution when seas begin to increase.

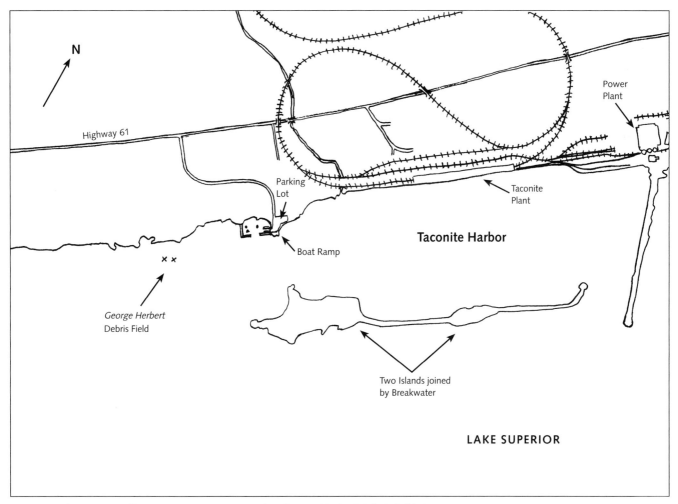

Map 33: A boat ramp offers convenient access to the *George Herbert* debris field site. Drawn by Stephen B. Daniel.

The logging tools and other metal artifacts are scattered across the bottom among the rocks. The freight scow was battered by the fierce storm, breaking apart immediately after it was heaved onto the rocky shore by the huge waves. The timbers were strewn along the shore, leaving nothing of the vessel to be seen on the bottom.

Fig. 286 (right): The Taconite Harbor Boat Ramp offers convenient access to the *George Herbert* debris field. The site is also part of the Safe Harbor program, with three mooring buoys available for different sizes of boats. Photo by Stephen B. Daniel.

Fig. 287: Shovels that were intended for the lumber camps are strewn across the bottom where the scow wrecked. Courtesy of Elmer Engman, Proctor, Minnesota.

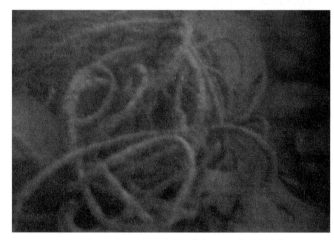

Fig. 288: A cable is also part of the debris at the wreck site. Courtesy of Elmer Engman, Proctor, Minnesota.

Point of Interest in Lake Superior at Tofte

America Dock

Tofte was a busy site for commercial fishing at the turn of the twentieth century. A large fishing business operated from a twin building near the edge of the bay. A dock constructed of concrete on top of cribbing was built nearby to provide easier access to the steamship *America*, which picked up passengers, delivered mail, and transferred fish and other freight. The ship was the primary link to Duluth, Port Arthur, and Fort William, as well as Isle Royale.

The dock can still be seen from the shoreline of the bay today, extending out into Lake Superior from behind the Bluefin Bay Resort. It is no longer usable, since time and storms have taken their toll. The North Shore Commercial Fishing Museum is located near the former site of the building that once housed the fishing operation. (For information on the Grand Marais dock used by the *America*, see pp. 159–60.) Several historic artifacts from the *America* are on display at the museum. In addition to a history of the commercial fishing that took place in this area, the museum offers a perspective on the *America*, which provided a vital communication and shipping service to the people who lived and worked along the North Shore of Lake Superior. The *America* sank at Isle Royale in 1928. Thom Holden and I wrote a book detailing this event and the shipwreck, *S.S. America: A Diver's Vision of the Past*, which is available at the museum.

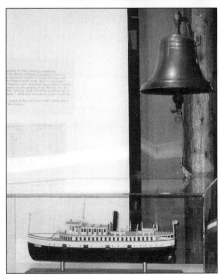

Fig. 289 (above): The remains of the *America* dock behind the Bluefin Bay Resort. Photo by Stephen B. Daniel.

Fig. 290 (above left): The *America* loads passengers and freight at the dock in Tofte. Courtesy of Betty Lessard/Brian Tofte Collection, Lake Superior Maritime Collection, University of Wisconsin–Superior.

Fig. 291 (left): The *America*'s bell was donated to the North Shore Commercial Fishing museum in 2001. It is on display with a model of the ship. Photo by Stephen B. Daniel.

Shipwrecks in Lake Superior at Grand Marais

Elgin

The *Elgin* was built as a lumber schooner-barge at the Louis Schickluna shipyard, located on the banks of the Welland Canal at St. Catherines in Ontario, Canada.[93] The three-masted schooner was 139 feet long, with a beam of 25.8 feet and a 12-foot depth of hold, and grossed 330 tons. The small schooner was launched at St. Catherines in April 1874 and plied the Great Lakes under the Canadian flag for many years.

The schooner had a rough time with a fierce storm in Lake Michigan in August 1885. With extremely poor visibility, the ship's crew could not see the shoreline as they sailed in the heavy seas. The *Elgin* was driven aground on the sandy bottom by wind and waves off Racine, Wisconsin. Water washed over the decks as the crew sought shelter in the cabin and forecastle. It took another day before the seas subsided enough for the captain to order a boat launched and head toward shore to seek help. He took a

train to Chicago, where a wrecking tug was enlisted to help free the ship.[94]

After the insurance company authorized salvage, the tug was dispatched with several large pumps to remove the water from the *Elgin*'s hold. It took more pumps to lighten the vessel before it could be towed to deeper water. Canvas had to be wrapped around the hull to keep the ship afloat, since the beating waves had opened its seams, allowing sand to sift inside. The ship was abandoned by its owners in Chicago following a damage assessment. It was sold by the U.S. marshal to pay for salvage expenses. The ship was eventually recaulked, repaired, and returned to service on the Great Lakes under the U.S. flag.

The *Elgin* carried lumber for a number of years afterward, with a carrying capacity of 330,000 board feet. It was outfitted with steam pumps in 1902 and had its bottom recaulked. In 1905, it was unrigged and used as a barge; its new home port was Duluth.

Fig. 292: The schooner *Elgin* with full sails during its early years. Courtesy of Great Lakes Marine Collection, Milwaukee Public Library / Wisconsin Marine Historical Society.

THE SINKING

In 1906 the *Elgin* was being towed by the tug *Crosby*, heading for Chicago after departing Duluth. Its cargo consisted of coal and hay. As the ships passed the Cross River, the *Elgin*'s hull began to leak. The pumps had difficulty keeping up with the flooding occurring below deck, so the two vessels headed for shelter in the harbor of Grand Marais. But by the time they reached the entrance to the harbor, the *Elgin*'s deck was awash. The *Elgin* struck bottom as the ships entered the harbor, and it was unable to move.[95] Its low position in the water made it vulnerable to wave actions, and a strong northeast wind was producing high seas that washed over the ship. The tugboat captain applied for permission to abandon the ship, as he thought it would be broken up in the rising storm. There are no records of salvage attempts after this incident.[96]

THE SHIPWRECK

Tidewater Atlantic Research did an extensive search in July 1992 in an attempt to find the remains of the wooden hull of the *Elgin*. All they found were three iron knees, the largest being 4 feet 8.5 inches on the long side and 2 feet 7.5 inches on the short. The other two knees were slightly smaller. The iron knees were representative of the type used on Canadian ships of that time. No wooden remains were found. A U.S. Army Corps of Engineers map of the harbor from the 1930s depicts a shipwreck near the outer side of the breakwater, which today protects the marina inside the harbor.

DIVING THE *ELGIN* SHIPWRECK

Type of Vessel	Wooden schooner-barge
Location	Grand Marais harbor, on west side, off shore from the picnic shelter
Depth	10 feet
Dive Rating	Novice diver

This dive is accessible from shore, although there is also a nearby boat ramp. The picnic shelter offers a convenient place to dress, as there are several picnic tables available. Enter the water from the beach, and swim northeast to the dive site, which starts about seventy-five feet offshore. Be aware of boat traffic in the harbor, and use a divers-down flag.

At the time I dove this site, the iron knees were chained to a rectangular metal hatch combing located slightly northeast of the picnic shelter area in eight to ten feet of water. No wooden remains of this ship have been found to date, although some divers in the past have reported a ship's ribs in the harbor.

Fig. 294: An anchor typical of the type used by schooners is on display outside of the North House Folk School. Photo by Stephen B. Daniel.

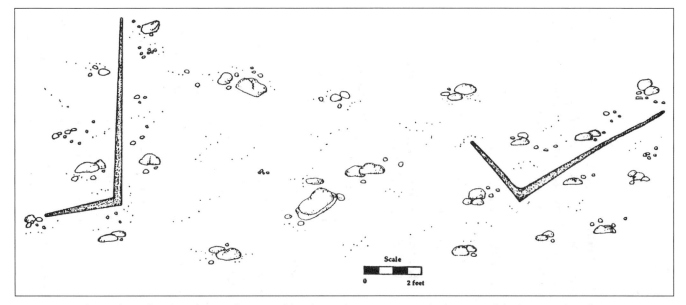

Fig. 293: Iron knees from the *Elgin* shipwreck. A metal hatch combing is now attached to one of the knees with a chain. Drawing by Tidewater Atlantic Research, courtesy of Minnesota Historical Society / State Historic Preservation Office.

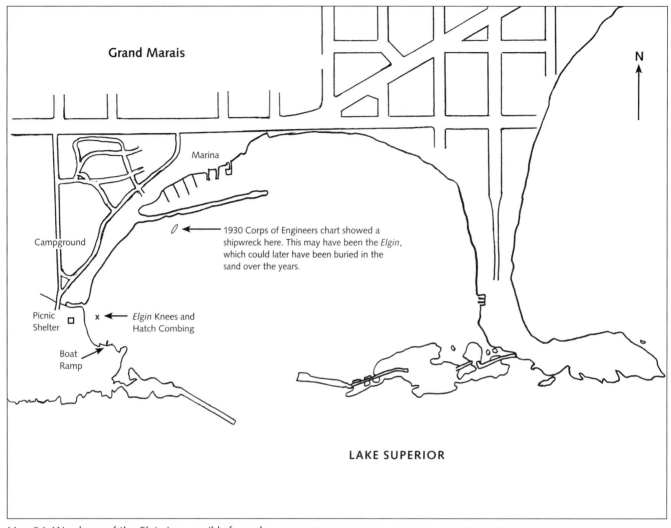

Map 34: **Wreckage of the *Elgin* is accessible from shore.** Drawn by Stephen B. Daniel, based on *Richardsons' Chartbook and Cruising Guide: Lake Superior.*

Fig. 295: Boat ramp in Grand Marais, near the city's campgrounds. Picnic shelter is in the background, on the left. Divers may enter from the beach to swim to the *Elgin*'s iron knees. Photo by Stephen B. Daniel.

Within map 34 (labels):
Grand Marais

N

Marina

1930 Corps of Engineers chart showed a shipwreck here. This may have been the *Elgin*, which could later have been buried in the sand over the years.

Campground

Picnic Shelter

x ← *Elgin* Knees and Hatch Combing

Boat Ramp

LAKE SUPERIOR

Liberty

The *Liberty* was a wooden steamer built on the Fox River and launched at Fort Howard, Wisconsin, on April 23, 1889. It was 96.8 feet long, with a beam of 18 feet and a depth of hold of 5.5 feet, and grossed 95.53 tons. Power came from a single-cylinder engine built by John Duncan that was high-pressure and noncondensing and had automatic expansion. The operational speed was 125 rpm, producing 150 horsepower.[97]

The small ship had a single boiler 9 feet long and 5.5 feet in diameter, with an operating pressure of 109 psi. A pair of sidewheels were powered by this engine and boiler, with an estimated speed of twenty miles per hour. Passenger and crew accommodations were built below deck, with future plans to build a more elegant cabin above deck. The early operations of the *Liberty* took place around the Sturgeon Bay area. The ship caught fire at Green Bay on August 11, 1889, as a result of sparks from passing ships.

The *Liberty* was rebuilt as a propeller in early 1891, increasing its capacity to 143.5 gross tons. In 1917, it was rebuilt again in Duluth, then rebuilt a fourth and final time in 1918. Its final gross tonnage was 149.86. The *Liberty* carried passengers and freight on Lake Superior after 1895, making different scheduled runs on Lake Superior. These included two-day runs to the Apostle Islands as well as four-day trips along the North Shore and to Isle Royale.

Fig. 296: The *Liberty* featured in an advertisement in the June 30, 1917, edition of the *Duluth Herald*. Courtesy of Minnesota Historical Society.

Fig. 297: The *Liberty* about 1902 at Sault Ste. Marie. Photo by A. E. Young, courtesy of C. Patrick Labadie Collection, Superior, Wisconsin.

The ship had many owners over the years, including A. Booth Packing Company and a series of owners from places in southwestern Michigan, such as Holland, Douglas, and Saugatuck. Several of the owners served as its captain. J. M. Clow and D. D. Clow bought the *Liberty* in June 1911 and kept the ship until 1917, when John H. Clow of the Scandia Fish Company of Duluth purchased it.

THE SINKING

The *Liberty* caught fire while tied to the dock in the harbor of Grand Marais on Sunday night, July 6, 1919. The ship burned to the waterline, totally destroying the vessel. The intense fire also consumed the dock and two houses on shore. No attempt to salvage the vessel was made.

THE SHIPWRECK

No large sections of the ship's hull remain. Two sections of the hull (a piece of the bow and a side section) may be observed off the north side of the concrete breakwater. Otherwise, most of the wreckage is located below the natural rocky section of the south breakwater on the harbor side. Many metal artifacts and small pieces of charred wood are located in the debris field there. The rudder is the most undamaged piece of the ship that is left today. It may easily be seen in shallow water near the beach on the west side of the harbor, within sight of the picnic shelter.

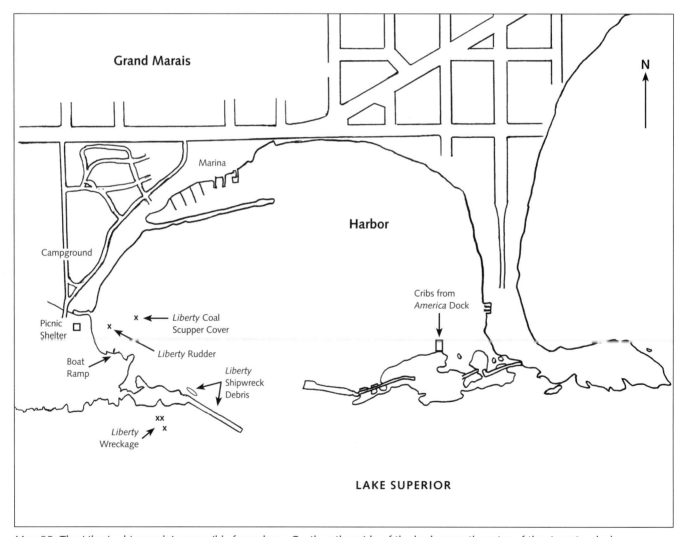

Map 35: The *Liberty* shipwreck is accessible from shore. On the other side of the harbor are the ruins of the *America* dock (see p. 159–60). Drawn by Stephen B. Daniel, based on *Richardsons' Chartbook and Cruising Guide: Lake Superior*.

DIVING THE *LIBERTY*

Type of Vessel	Wooden steamer
Location	Grand Marais harbor, at base of the natural breakwater on the south side
Depth	15 feet
Dive Rating	Novice diver

This dive is accessible from shore. Enter to the south of the boat ramp, and swim toward the natural breakwater rock. Because of boats moving inside the harbor, be sure to use a divers-down flag.

Drop down to about twelve feet, and look for debris from the burned ship. Visibility is about fifteen feet. The capstan rests in the rocks. Several other metal pieces may also be observed: pipes, heavy iron pieces with curved edges, iron straps with charred wood attached, pumps, T-fittings, and several other items. The thirteen-foot bow section is 150 feet from the north end of the concrete breakwater on the west side of the harbor, at a twenty-foot depth. A seven-foot section of the hull side planks are located in about twenty feet of water north of the bow section. The rudder may be found offshore from the beach by the picnic shelter in about five feet of water, not too far from the iron knees of the *Elgin*. More wreckage is near the lake side of the breakwater.

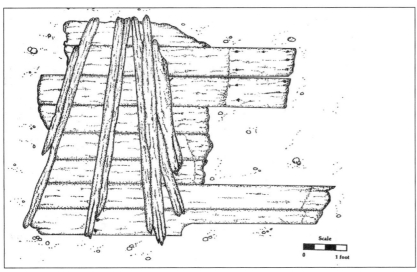

Fig. 298: Section of planking with frames from the *Liberty*. Drawing by Tidewater Atlantic Research, courtesy of Minnesota Historical Society / State Historic Preservation Office.

Fig. 299: The south natural breakwater. The wreckage of the *Liberty* begins at the base of this rocky formation in about twelve feet of water. Photo by Stephen B. Daniel.

Fig. 300: **Bow section of the *Liberty* shipwreck.** Courtesy of Minnesota Historical Society / State Historic Preservation Office.

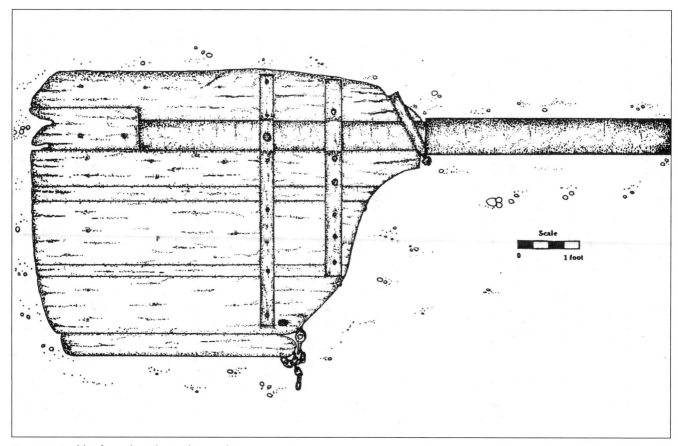

Fig. 301: **Rudder from the *Liberty* shipwreck.** Drawing by Tidewater Atlantic Research, courtesy of Minnesota Historical Society / State Historic Preservation Office.

Point of Interest in Lake Superior at Grand Marais

America Dock

The steamship *America* stopped often in Grand Marais on its trips up and down the North Shore between Canada, Isle Royale, and Duluth. The ship docked on the east side of the harbor to pick up passengers, and fish from the local fishermen. After the *America* sank at Isle Royale in 1928, passenger service shifted from ships to automobiles. Consequently the dock in the harbor deteriorated over time. Today only cribs remain (see map 35, p. 156); you can see them extending from the rocky section of the southeast breakwater. (For information on the Tofte dock used by the *America*, see p. 151.)

The Cook County Historical Society, located in the

Fig. 302: The *America* made regular stops at Grand Marais during the early part of the twentieth century. Photo by Hugh McKenzie (May 1910), courtesy of Lake Superior Maritime Collection, University of Wisconsin–Superior.

lighthouse keeper's house on the east side of the harbor, maintains a museum that includes a display of several photographs of the *America* as well as some artifacts from the ship. The wheel is one of the artifacts; it was re-covered from the backyard of a local resident many years ago and carefully restored to excellent condition.

Fig. 303: The wheel from the *America* ship-wreck in Lake Superior near Isle Royale. Photo by Stephen B. Daniel.

Ship Gone Missing in Lake Superior near Brule River

Mary Martini

The *Mary Martini* was built as a steam packet at the F. W. Wheeler shipyard at West Bay City, Michigan, in 1877.[98] The small steamer was eighty-five feet long and grossed ninety-six tons. In the summer of 1883, the ship was brought to Duluth by L. F. Johnson and James Bardon to serve as a ferry between Duluth and Superior.[99] It was later sold to Captain Joseph Lloyd of Duluth. In addition to carrying passengers, the *Martini* collected fish at different points along the North Shore and delivered them to the cities at the western end of Lake Superior.

THE SINKING

December 23, 1885, brought fair weather on the big lake. The visibility was good, but the *Mary Martini* still ran into problems. Apparently, faulty navigation caused the small ship to run aground about sixteen miles northeast of Grand Marais at Brule Point. The passengers and crew of the *Martini* were removed safely and brought to Duluth by the tug *T. H. Camp*. The tug also salvaged a 3,500-pound cargo of fish, which it delivered to Duluth for the *Martini* operators.

To date, no remains of the sunken two-decker wooden steamer have been found. It is likely that the small steamship broke apart during winter storms and was swept away piece by piece over the years.

Fig. 304: The passenger steamer *Mary Martini*. Courtesy of St. Louis County Historical Society Collection, Duluth, Minnesota.

Ship Gone Missing in Lake Superior at Susie Island, Grand Portage

Isle Royale

The *Isle Royale* was built as a passenger and package freight steamer in 1879. Originally built under the name of *Agnes*, it was launched at Port Huron, Michigan.[100] The steamer was ninety-one feet in length and grossed fifty-five tons. The ship was purchased by Cooley, LaVaque and Company and brought to Duluth in 1884.[101] Their intention was to provide a passenger and package freight service along the North Shore of Lake Superior.

THE SINKING

The *Isle Royale* met its end on July 27, 1885, northwest of its namesake in Lake Superior. The steamer struck bottom during a minor storm and sprang a leak while sailing near Susie Island, on the eastern edge of Waus-wau-goning Bay, just northeast of Grand Portage. All of the passengers and crew escaped safely to Susie Island, while the small steamer sank southwest of the island.

There is no report of salvage, and no one has found the remains of the ship. It is doubtful that much wreckage would be visible after many years and damage caused by ice at shallow depths.

Fig. 305: The packet steamer *Isle Royale*. Courtesy of Julius Wolff Collection.

Shipwreck in Lake Superior at Victoria Island, Canada

Howard

The *Howard*, a wooden steamer, started its life on water as the *Admiral D. D. Porter*. It was built in 1864 at Wilmington, Delaware, under the authorization of the Lincoln administration during the Civil War.[102] It was 115 foot long and grossed 195 tons.[103] Its large steam engine was a single-cylinder compound type. Pressure from the steam pushed the large piston both up and down. This was a different method of operation from most steam engines, which rely on a flywheel to move the piston back to the top of its stroke. The compound engine performed two power strokes on each revolution.[104]

The *Porter* spent its first year as a gunboat patrolling the East Coast and South America. It wore a number of other names as an ocean-going tug before becoming the *Howard* and steaming into Lake Superior. The *Howard* was the oldest vessel to be operating on Lake Superior at the time of its loss.

Fig. 307: The tug *Howard*. Courtesy of Great Lakes Marine Collection, Milwaukee Public Library / Wisconsin Marine Historical Society.

THE SINKING

On June 13, 1921, the *Howard* ran aground on the north side of the reef at the west end of Victoria Island, southwest of Thunder Bay. After rowing a lifeboat to shore at Cloud Bay, the first mate hiked along Highway 61 to get help. A tug was dispatched to the stranded ship. As the tug started to pull the *Howard* off the reef, the ship sank at the stern and went down to the bottom. Another account says a fire took place before it sank.[105] Evidence from the wreck shows that it was not damaged very badly by fire; most of the structure is still present (although the ship has partially collapsed upon itself).

THE SHIPWRECK

This shipwreck rests in Canadian waters, a little over seventeen miles northeast of Grand Portage. The *Howard* is lying on its starboard side, with the stern section facing in a west-east position and the keel facing toward the upper part of the reef. The bow section is separated from the rear part of the hull and points north, and the rudder is located immediately north of the propeller at the stern. The ship is partially collapsed, with the big single-cylinder engine seeming to spill out of the hull toward the bottom. The boiler is located alongside the east side of the engine. Some coal is still visible inside.

Fig. 306: The *Howard* awaiting another day's work on the lake. Courtesy of Great Lakes Marine Collection, Milwaukee Public Library / Wisconsin Marine Historical Society.

DIVING THE *HOWARD*

Type of Vessel	Wooden steamer
Location	Victoria Island, Ontario, Canada, at the base of the north side of the reef on the west end of the island
GPS Coordinates	48°04.858′ N, 89°21.765′ W
Depth	92 feet
Dive Rating	Advanced diver

This dive is accessible only from a boat. The nearest boat launch is at the Grand Portage Marina, seventeen miles south of Victoria Island. Do not tie up to a nearby navigation buoy, but instead anchor off the reef (approximate nearby depth is sixty-five feet). Be aware of the flat, rocky bottom as well as northwest winds that could move the boat toward the reef. Since this shipwreck is located in Canadian waters, any disembarking on shore will require a reporting visit to the Customs Office.

The shipwreck is located at the bottom of the reef. Swimming around the large engine suspended outside the hull makes this dive memorable.

Fig. 308: **The wreck of the tug** *Howard*. Drawing by Stephen B. Daniel.

Fig. 309: **The** *Howard*'s large propeller. Courtesy of Terry Flynn, Minneapolis, Minnesota.

Fig. 310: **Wreckage of the** *Howard*. Courtesy of Terry Flynn, Minneapolis, Minnesota.

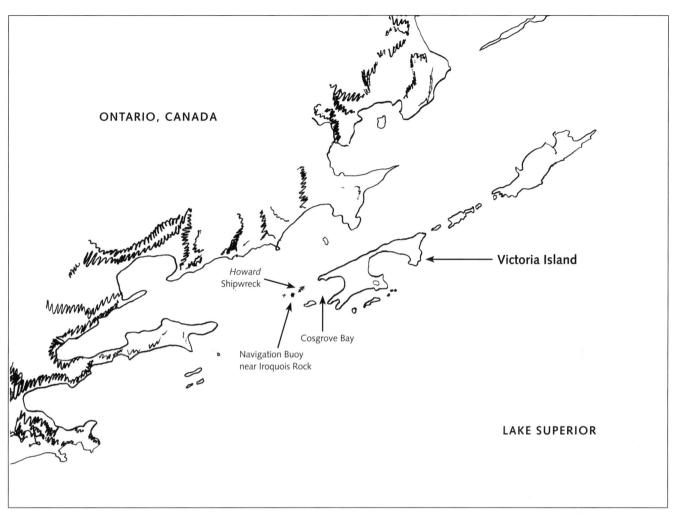

ONTARIO, CANADA

Howard
Shipwreck

Cosgrove Bay

Navigation Buoy
near Iroquois Rock

← Victoria Island

LAKE SUPERIOR

Map 36: The *Howard* shipwreck is located in Canadian waters, near Victoria Island. Drawn by Stephen B. Daniel, based on *Richardsons' Chartbook and Cruising Guide: Lake Superior.*

Fig. 311: The engine of the *Howard*. Courtesy of Ken Merryman, Fridley, Minnesota.

Proposal
for an Intentional Sinking

MANY SCUBA DIVERS who visit the Minnesota North Shore have expressed an interest in having an additional shipwreck to dive that would offer more to see than many of the existing shipwrecks. The Great Lakes Shipwreck Preservation Society (GLSPS) has also been approached by several dive shops that would help support an effort to add another ship to the North Shore dive site selection. The Minnesota Department of Natural Resources (DNR) conducted meetings several years ago to solicit interest from the diving community regarding the potential for intentionally sinking a ship in Lake Superior along the North Shore. Benefits include alleviating diver activity on many of the historic shipwrecks along the North Shore and contributions to the local economy by visiting divers.

In June 1999, the GLSPS conducted a trial sinking of a thirty-seven-foot ferro-cement sailboat to determine what would be involved in the process of sinking a boat or a ship in Lake Superior (see pp. 117–19). Many other large vessels have been intentionally sunk near Florida, North Carolina, California, Washington, and Canada. Divers Unlimited, Inc., a drysuit manufacturer, led the effort to sink the Canadian navy cruiser *Yukon* in the Pacific Ocean near San Diego. Their process encountered difficulties along the way but was successful. A brief synopsis may be helpful in understanding what may be involved in an intentional sinking.

A nonprofit organization was created to manage and fund the process. It raised money to acquire the ship, transport it to San Diego, and remove hazardous chemicals. Dockage was obtained from the City of San Diego to store the ship during the preparation process. Hundreds of volunteers helped to remove doors or weld them, cut new large openings at each deck level for easy diver access, apply labels to the openings to identify where the diver was positioned on the ship, and pull miles of wires out to avoid potential entanglement. The preparation took over seven thousand hours to complete. When the

ship was towed toward the designated sinking site, it encountered problems with increasing seas, but it still sank near the intended location. The shipwreck has become the most popular scuba diving site on the West Coast and draws visitors from around the world. The shipwreck is also used for training exercises by different government organizations.

The U.S. government has determined that a huge number of ships currently in storage will soon be outliving their potential usefulness, should the need arise in a national emergency to call them back into service. The government would typically consider sending the ships out to be scrapped to resolve the issue of this obsolete floating equipment, but scrapping such a large number is not financially feasible. A government study recommended creating a program to offer the ships to organizations that could use them as artificial reefs to develop new fish habitats and as recreational attractions for scuba divers and anglers. As a result, the Maritime Administration of the U.S. Department of Transportation created a program for the benefit of scuba divers.[106]

The Diving Equipment and Marketing Association is sponsoring the Ships to Reefs program to help local groups obtain a U.S. military surplus vessel before it would be scrapped. The federal government will donate a qualifying ship to a recognized nonprofit that can fulfill the requirements to transport, prepare, and sink the vessel with the approval of local government agencies. The government will also provide a grant to have the vessel cleaned.

The GLSPS is investigating the possibility of sinking a retired commercial bulk freighter. The objective would be to prepare and sink the ship in Lake Superior, in a place where diver access would be available from shore and by boat. Facilities for diver access would need to be provided as part of the project. Because of the size of the ships that have been considered, a hundred-foot depth would be required to sink the ship in navigable waters. One of the biggest obstacles is the substantial financial resources needed to acquire, transport, and prepare the ship. The GLSPS hopes that both divers and nondivers would be interested in supporting this project, which would benefit the diving community and others.

About the Great Lakes Shipwreck Preservation Society

The Great Lakes Shipwreck Preservation Society was founded in 1996 by a group of Minnesota divers who were interested in stabilizing and preserving shipwrecks in the Great Lakes region. Many of the founders had been diving in Lake Superior for over twenty-five years and had noticed the gradual deterioration of many shipwrecks. Although this is a natural and ongoing process, they thought that something should be done to slow it down. They wanted their children who were divers to be able to enjoy diving the same shipwrecks in the future.

The society is a nonprofit, tax-exempt organization whose members come from all walks of life. Most are divers, historians, and those who enjoy the lore of shipwrecks. All have a vision of preserving these underwater treasures, which bring excitement and fascination to those who observe them underwater or in photographs and video footage.

The society has been involved with several projects on the Minnesota North Shore, including monitoring and stabilizing the *Samuel P. Ely* shipwreck in Agate Bay. The GLSPS also installed a mooring buoy for dive boats near the *Ely* in 2001. The GLSPS installs and removes mooring buoys annually on the *Madeira*, the *Hesper*, and the *Just for Fun* shipwrecks, and it has completed extensive documentation of both the *Ely* and the *Hesper*. The GLSPS has also provided assistance to maritime history organizations in the Apostle Islands and Milwaukee.

The GLSPS conducts training classes to teach underwater documentation that includes triangulation and drawing. Other classes teach how to work with tools underwater and assemble structures underwater. The GLSPS also sponsors safety, first aid, CPR, oxygen provider, and automatic external defibrillator classes taught by skilled professionals.

Educational programs about preserving shipwrecks, with slide shows and videos, are presented to interested groups, including schools, dive certification classes, Explorer Scouts, and the Rotary Club. The GLSPS sponsors Dive into the Past, an annual educational program on maritime history, shipwrecks, and different types of diving, on the last Saturday of February each year.

If you would like to learn more about the GLSPS, please visit its website at: http://www.glsps.org.

All proceeds from this book after expenses will be donated to the GLSPS to support its various programs.

Notes

Shipwreck in the St. Louis River at Oliver, Wisconsin

1. David D. Swayze, *Shipwreck! A Comprehensive Directory of Over 3,700 Shipwrecks on the Great Lakes: Includes the Most Dangerous Spot on the Lakes, Largest Freighters Lost, the Most Dangerous Decade, Treasure Ships* (Boyne City, MI: Harbor House, 1992), 166.

2. Julius F. Wolff Jr., *Lake Superior Shipwrecks*, ed. Thomas R. Holden, 2nd expanded ed. (Duluth, MN: Lake Superior Port Cities, 1990), 132.

Shipwrecks in the St. Louis River at Duluth

3. Swayze, *Shipwreck!* 250.
4. Wolff, *Lake Superior Shipwrecks*, 34.
5. Swayze, *Shipwreck!* 250.
6. Wolff, *Lake Superior Shipwrecks*, 64.

Shipwrecks in Lake Superior at Duluth, Part 1

7. Anna L. Bovia, *Camp Perry 1906–1991* (Defiance, Ohio: Hubbard, 1992), 72.

8. Scott F. Anfinson, "*U.S.S. Essex*: Description of the Wreck Event," Lake Superior Shipwrecks, Minnesota Historical Society, http://www.mnhs.org/places /nationalregister/shipwrecks/essex/essdwe.html.

9. *Richardsons' Chartbook and Cruising Guide: Lake Superior* (Gaylord, MI: Richardsons' Marine, 2001), 23.

10. John Meyers, "Mystery from the Deep," *Duluth News Tribune*, February 21, 2007.

11. Steve Daniel and Jay Hanson, "Shipwreck off Minnesota Point Identified," *Great Lakes Shipwreck Preservation Society Newsletter* (Spring 2007): 4.

12. Swayze, *Shipwreck!* 189.
13. Wolff, *Lake Superior Shipwrecks*, 43.
14. Swayze, *Shipwreck!* 146.

15. Wolff, *Lake Superior Shipwrecks*, 116.

16. Paul Hancock, *Shipwrecks of the Great Lakes* (San Diego: Thunder Bay, 2004), 49.

17. Megan Long, *Disaster: Great Lakes* (Toronto: Lynx Images, 2002), 13.

18. Lee Alfred Opheim, "Twentieth Century Shipwrecks in Lake Superior" (PhD diss., St. Louis University, 1971), 297.

19. Albin Jackman, "Eighty Ships to the Sea," *Telescope* 18, no. 5 (1969): 123.

Historic Artifacts in Lake Superior at Duluth

20. Downtown Lakewalk plaque, Duluth, Minnesota.
21. Endion Station plaque, Duluth, Minnesota.

22. Elmer Engman, "The Old Duluth Harbor," *Underwater* (newsletter by Innerspace Scuba, Inc.) 1, no. 1 (October 2004): 1.

Shipwrecks in Lake Superior at Duluth, Part 2

23. Elmer Engman, "Whaleback *Thomas Wilson*: A Centennial Remembrance," *Nor'Easter* [Duluth, Minnesota] (March–April 2002): 1–6.

24. For more about the *Wilson* sinking, see Elmer Engman, *In the Belly of a Whale: Duluth's Shipwreck Tragedy* (Duluth, MN: Innerspace, 1988).

25. Jennifer L. Moravchik, "*Thomas Wilson*: Whaleback," *Nor'Easter* [Duluth, Minnesota] (March–April 2002): 6–9.

26. Engman, *In the Belly of a Whale*, 19.

27. Tidewater Atlantic Research, "An Underwater Archaeological Assessment of the Steam Tug *A. C. Adams* and Bulk Freighter *Onoko* and Surveys for the Bulk Freighter *Benjamin Noble* and Schooner *Charlie* in Lake Superior near Duluth, Minnesota," June 25, 1991, in *Archaeological and Historical Studies of Minnesota's Lake*

Superior Shipwrecks, ed. Scott F. Anfinson (St. Paul: State Historic Preservation Office, Minnesota Historical Society, 1993), 2–13.

28. Wolff, *Lake Superior Shipwrecks*, 66.

29. Ibid., 63.

Underwater Geology, Part 1

30. Steve Harrington with David J. Cooper, *Divers Guide to Wisconsin: Including Minnesota's North Shore* (Mason, MI: Maritime, 1991), 184.

31. Ibid., 185.

32. Swayze, *Shipwreck!* 179.

33. Wolff, *Lake Superior Shipwrecks*, 154.

Shipwrecks in Lake Superior near Knife Island

34. Tidewater Atlantic Research, "Underwater Archaeological Assessment," 13–14.

35. James Barry, *Ships of the Great Lakes: 300 Years of Navigation*, (Holt, MI: Thunder Bay, 1996), 136.

36. Wolff, *Lake Superior Shipwrecks*, 155.

37. Swayze, *Shipwreck!* 92.

38. Randolph Beebe, *Thomas Friant Timeline*, 2004, 1–2 (unpublished manuscript).

39. Wolff, *Lake Superior Shipwrecks*, 152.

40. Tidewater Atlantic Research, "Underwater Archaeological Assessment," in *Archaeological and Historical Studies,* ed. Anfinson, 29–37.

41. Kenneth Merryman, "*Benjamin Noble*: The Legend of the North Shore," *Great Lakes Shipwreck Preservation Society Newsletter* (Fall 2005): 2.

42. *Duluth Herald*, April 29, 1914.

43. Larry Oakes, "Legend Yields to Truth with Wreck's Discovery," *Star Tribune*, July 20, 2005, A5.

44. Wolff, *Lake Superior Shipwrecks*, 102–3.

45. Swayze, *Shipwreck!* 138.

Point of Interest in Lake Superior at Knife River

46. Harrington, *Divers Guide to Wisconsin*, 187.

47. Frank A. King, *Minnesota Logging Railroads* (Minneapolis: University of Minnesota Press, 2003), 70–71.

Shipwreck in Lake Superior near Knife River

48. Swayze, *Shipwreck!* 106.

49. Wolff, *Lake Superior Shipwrecks*, 152.

Shipwrecks in Lake Superior near Two Harbors

50. Swayze, *Shipwreck!* 106.

51. Wolff, *Lake Superior Shipwrecks*, 152.

52. Chuck Frederick, "Looking into the Watery Grave," *Duluth News Tribune*, November 10, 2005.

53. Scott F. Anfinson, "*Samuel Ely*: Description of the Wreck Event," Lake Superior Shipwrecks, Minnesota Historical Society, http://www.mnhs.org/places/nationalregister/shipwrecks/ely/elydwe.html.

54. Wolff, *Lake Superior Shipwrecks*, 152.

Underwater Geology, Part 2

55. Cris Kohl, *The Great Lakes Diving Guide* (West Chicago, IL: Seawolf Communications, 2001), 377.

56. Harrington, *Divers Guide to Wisconsin*, 187.

Shipwreck in Lake Superior near Encampment Island

57. Swayze, *Shipwreck!* 106.

58. Tidewater Atlantic Research, "Underwater Documentation at Grand Marais Harbor," January 14, 1993, in *Archaeological and Historical Studies*, ed. Anfinson.

59. Edward J. Dowling, "The Tin Stackers," *Inland Seas* (Summer 1953): 278.

60. Wolff, *Lake Superior Shipwrecks*, 114.

61. Hancock, *Shipwrecks of the Great Lakes*, 52.

Ship Gone Missing in Lake Superior near Encampment Island

62. Swayze, *Shipwreck!* 35.

63. Wolff, *Lake Superior Shipwrecks*, 22.

64. Duane R. Lund, *The North Shore of Lake Superior, Yesterday and Today* (Staples, MN: Nordell Graphic Communications, 1995), 69.

Historic Artifacts in Lake Superior at Gooseberry River

65. Swayze, *Shipwreck!* 63.

66. Wolff, *Lake Superior Shipwrecks*, 99.

Shipwreck in Lake Superior at Split Rock Island

67. Wolff, *Lake Superior Shipwrecks*, 85.

Historic Artifacts in Lake Superior at Split Rock River

68. Tidewater Atlantic Research, "A Cultural Resources Survey along the North Shore of Lake Superior between East Beaver Bay and Castle Danger, Minnesota," in *Archaeological and Historical Studies*, ed. Anfinson, 32.

69. Ibid.

Shipwreck in Lake Superior at Gold Rock Point

70. Swayze, *Shipwreck!* 35.

71. Brina J. Agranat, Stephen R. James Jr., and Kevin J. Foster, Panamerican Consultants, "Submerged Cultural Resources Investigation, Shipwrecks *Madeira* and *Thomas Wilson*, Lake Superior, Minnesota," in *Archaeological and Historical Studies*, ed. Anfinson, 16–17.

72. "News of the Lakes," *Duluth Herald*, June 7, 1902.

73. Wolff, *Lake Superior Shipwrecks*, 114.

74. Ibid.

75. Agranat, James, and Foster, Panamerican Consultants, "Submerged Cultural Resources," 39.

Historic Artifact in Lake Superior near Beaver Bay

76. Tidewater Atlantic Research, "Underwater Archaeological Assessment," in *Archaeological and Historical Studies*, ed. Anfinson, 43–46.

77. Jessie C. Davis, *Beaver Bay: Original North Shore Village* (Duluth, MN: Bay Area Historical Society and St. Louis County Historical Society, 1968), 70.

78. Tidewater Atlantic Research, "Underwater Archaeological Assessment," in *Archaeological and Historical Studies*, ed. Anfinson, 46–47.

Shipwrecks in Lake Superior at Silver Bay

79. Panamerican Consultants, "National Register Assessment of Four Great Lakes Shipwrecks: The *Essex*, *Hesper*, *Amboy* and *George Spencer*, Lake Superior, Minnesota," in *Archaeological and Historical Studies*, ed. Anfinson, 12.

80. Wolff, *Lake Superior Shipwrecks*, 105.

81. Elmer Engman, "Steamer *Hesper*: Grinding Death," *Nordic Diver* 3 (1975).

82. Swayze, *Shipwreck!* 92.

83. Wolff, *Lake Superior Shipwrecks*, 240.

84. Hancock, *Shipwrecks of the Great Lakes*, 138.

Shipwrecks in Lake Superior at Thomasville

85. Panamerican Consultants, "National Register Assessment," in *Archaeological and Historical Studies*, ed. Anfinson, 19–20.

86. *Detroit Free Press*, December 1, 1905, 2.

87. *Duluth News Tribune*, December 6, 1905.

88. Panamerican Consultants, "National Register Assessment," in *Archaeological and Historical Studies*, ed. Anfinson, 16.

89. Ibid., 17.

Shipwreck in Lake Superior near Taconite Harbor

90. Swayze, *Shipwreck!* 108.

91. Wolff, *Lake Superior Shipwrecks*, 112–13.

92. Elmer Engman, *The Last Trip for the* George Herbert, Proctor, Minnesota, 2005, 3 (unpublished manuscript).

Shipwrecks in Lake Superior at Grand Marais

93. Tidewater Atlantic Research, "Underwater Documentation at Grand Marais Harbor, Minnesota, of the Schooner *Elgin*, and the Steamer *Liberty* and Nomination of the Steamer *Lafayette* and Rafting Tug *Niagara* to the National Register of Historic Places," in *Archaeological and Historical Studies*, ed. Anfinson, 22.

94. Ibid., 27.

95. Wolff, *Lake Superior Shipwrecks*, 120.

96. Tidewater Atlantic Research, "Underwater Documentation at Grand Marais Harbor," in *Archaeological and Historical Studies*, ed. Anfinson, 28.

97. Ibid., 3.

Ship Gone Missing in Lake Superior near Brule River

98. Swayze, *Shipwreck!* 144.

99. Wolff, *Lake Superior Shipwrecks*, 45.

Ship Gone Missing in Lake Superior at Susie Island, Grand Portage

100. Swayze, *Shipwreck!* 144.

101. Wolff, *Lake Superior Shipwrecks*, 42.

Shipwreck in Lake Superior at Victoria Island, Canada

102. Harold Rochat, "An 1864 Gunboat Sunk in Lake Superior," *Great Lakes Shipwreck Preservation Society Newsletter* (Fall 2000): 2.

103. Swayze, *Shipwreck!* 112.

104. Rochat, "1865 Gunboat Sunk," 2.

105. Wolff, *Lake Superior Shipwrecks*, 171.

Proposal for an Intentional Sinking

106. Steve Barsky, "Ships-to-Reefs Program," *Wreck Diving Magazine* 4 (Winter 2004): 67.

For Further Reading

Anfinson, Scott F., ed. *Archaeological and Historical Studies of Minnesota's Lake Superior Shipwrecks*. St. Paul: State Historic Preservation Office, Minnesota Historical Society, 1993.

Daniel, Stephen B., with Thom Holden. *S.S. America: A Diver's Vision of the Past*. Fridley, MN: Great Lakes Shipwreck Preservation Society, 2001.

Engman, Elmer. *In The Belly of a Whale: Duluth's Shipwreck Tragedy*. Duluth, MN: Innerspace, 1988.

Hancock, Paul. *Shipwrecks of the Great Lakes*. San Diego: Thunder Bay, 2004.

Harrington, Steve, with David J. Cooper. *Divers Guide to Wisconsin: Including Minnesota's North Shore*. Mason, MI: Maritime, 1991.

Kohl, Cris. *The Great Lakes Diving Guide*. West Chicago, IL: Seawolf Communications, 2001.

———. *The 100 Best Great Lakes Shipwrecks*. Volume 2: *Lake Michigan, Lake Superior*. West Chicago, IL: Seawolf Communications, 1998.

Lake Superior Shipwrecks. Minnesota Historical Society. http://www.mnhs.org/places/nationalregister/shipwrecks/essex/essdwe.html.

LesStrang, Jacques. *Cargo Carriers of the Great Lakes: The Saga of the Great Lakes Fleet—North America's Fresh Water Merchant Marine*. New York: American Legacy, 1985.

Long, Megan. *Disaster: Great Lakes*. Toronto: Lynx Images, 2002.

Lydecker, Ryck. *Pigboat: The Story of the Whalebacks*. Superior, WI: Sweetwater, 1981.

Marshall, James R. "Rewarding the Most *Noble* Discovery." *Lake Superior Magazine* 27, no. 4 (August–September 2005): 13–16.

Stonehouse, Frederick. *Went Missing: Unsolved Great Lakes Shipwreck Mysteries*. Gwinn, MI: Avery Color Studios, 2000.

Swayze, David D. *Shipwreck! A Comprehensive Directory of Over 3,700 Shipwrecks on the Great Lakes: Includes the Most Dangerous Spot on the Lakes, Largest Freighters Lost, the Most Dangerous Decade, Treasure Ships*. Boyne City, MI: Harbor House, 1992.

Wolff, Julius F., Jr. *Lake Superior Shipwrecks*. Edited by Thomas R. Holden. 2nd expanded ed. Duluth, MN: Lake Superior Port Cities, 1990.

Index

Please note: Italicized page numbers refer to photographs, drawings, maps, and other illustrations. All locations listed are in Minnesota unless otherwise specified.